TAKE ONE TIN

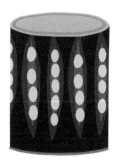

TAKE ONE TIN

80 DELICIOUS MEALS FROM THE STORECUPBOARD

Lola Milne

Photography by Lizzie Mayson

Kyle Books

An Hachette UK Company
www.hachette.co.uk

First published in Great Britain in 2020 by
Kyle Books, an imprint of Kyle Cathie Ltd
Carmelite House
50 Victoria Embankment
London EC4Y 0DZ
www.kylebooks.com

ISBN: 9780 85783 614 4

10 9 8 7 6 5 4 3 2 1

Publisher: Joanna Copestick
Editorial Director: Judith Hannam
Editor: Isabel Gonzalez-Prendergast
Photographer: Lizzie Mayson
Designer: Louise Leffler
Food stylist: Lola Milne
Prop stylist: Louie Waller
Illustrator: We are Out of Office
Production: Emily Noto

A Cataloguing in Publication record for this title
is available from the British Library.

Printed and bound in China

CONTENTS

INTRODUCTION

The storecupboard is a wondrous thing; I am always dipping in, whether to begin a meal, to embellish one or to create an entire dish. Within the storecupboard you will always find the humble tin – cheap, nutritious and long lasting. This book showcases these versatile creatures and gives you all sorts of new ideas on how to use them.

You can pick up a tin of tomatoes or tuna almost anywhere. The tin is universal, affordable and accessible. No need for snobbery: the tin is an undervalued resource. Every recipe in this book has something tinned at its core; from black beans to sardines or pears, each is the springboard for a quick, easy and delicious meal. Tinned food shouldn't be bland or dull; I hope to show you how to create new and exciting dishes from familiar tinned foods and introduce you to some lesser-used tinned friends-to-be.

Take One Tin is for people who want to inject some oomph into their Wednesday dinner, reinvent those storecupboard essentials and be introduced to some more unfamiliar ingredients that are just sitting on the shelf waiting to be discovered. Whether you're after a restorative breakfast or a yummy pudding, you'll find perfect recipes here all (pretty much) from the comfort of the tinned aisle.

The bulk of the ingredients used in support of the mighty tin are also from the storecupboard, meaning each recipe can be made without a shopping list as long as your arm; many recipes in the book have 10 ingredients or fewer. Storecupboard staples are topped up with fresh ingredients that can easily be found in most shops.

You'll notice that there isn't any meat in this book. I am no vegetarian, but I do see the importance of eating less meat for both environmental and health reasons. It has been great to get creative with vegetables, pulses and fish and not look to meat to be the centre of any dish. Of course, meat could be added to many of the dishes in this book, but I think they hold their own as they are. Hopefully you'll agree.

The chapters have been arranged to showcase the range of tins available, beginning with the staple that is beans and pulses. I am a true worshiper of the pulse. Tomatoes and vegetables come next, which play a central role in countless dishes. The book then goes on to the fish section, where I think you will be surprised at the range of delicious and affordable dishes you can make. The fruit and sweet tins chapter was heavily inspired by summers spent plodding about on my parents' allotment, helping them harvest, then watching them cooking and preserving their hauls of berries, pears and peaches. This chapter showcases the amazing tinned fruit you can get all year round, as well as things to make from storecupboard staples, like coconut milk. The final chapter provides you with a few tasty accompaniments to eat alongside your meal, all very simple and made using ingredients that are predominantly from your storecupboard.

A couple of practical bits: the oven temperatures are written for fan ovens; to convert to non-fan, simply add 20°C. There are a few recipes that either require or benefit from a stick blender or electric beaters; they are both great, small and cheap pieces of kit to have in your kitchen.

I hope this book helps you see how accessible, achievable – and often even joyous – cooking can be and to realise that it doesn't always need to be about fresh or expensive ingredients. My wish for this book is that it leads you to the conclusion that the tin is a wondrous thing.

BEANS & PULSES

SPICED CANNELLINI BEANS ON TOAST

Who doesn't love baked beans? These are a homemade alternative, sweet, spicy and warming. Top with a fried egg for a classic breakfast.

SERVES 2

1 tablespoon olive oil

1 garlic clove, finely chopped

¼ teaspoon chilli flakes

pinch of paprika

400g tin plum tomatoes

2 teaspoons Worcestershire sauce

1 teaspoon soft brown sugar

2 teaspoons cider vinegar

400g tin cannellini beans, drained and rinsed

salt and freshly ground black pepper

2 slices of bread

Heat the olive oil in a large frying pan over a low-medium heat. Once warm, add the garlic, fry until starting to turn golden, then add the spices and cook for a further 30 seconds. Tip in the plum tomatoes, Worcestershire sauce, sugar, vinegar and cannellini beans. Season, bring to the boil, then simmer on a medium-high heat for 15–20 minutes until slightly thickened.

Toast your bread and serve piled high with the beans, topped with a fried egg, if you like.

GREEN LENTIL FRITTERS

These are perfect for a lazy weekend brunch, try them with a fried egg. Beetroot can be swapped for parsnip or carrot (or pretty much any root veg).

SERVES 2 (ABOUT 6–8 FRITTERS)

400g tin green lentils, drained and rinsed

70g plain flour

1 egg, beaten

3 tablespoons chopped chives

1 teaspoon caraway seeds

1½ teaspoons paprika

1 garlic clove, finely chopped

200g raw beetroot, peeled and coarsely grated

1–2 tablespoons flavourless oil (such as sunflower)

salt and freshly ground black pepper

TO SERVE

1 teaspoon harissa

2 tablespoons natural yogurt

Mix together the lentils, flour, egg, chives, caraway seeds, paprika, garlic and beetroot, and then season.

Warm the oil in a large frying pan over a medium heat. For each fritter, dollop in a heaped tablespoon of mixture, flatten slightly and fry until golden (about 4 minutes per side). If they start to colour too soon, turn the heat down to low.

Meanwhile, mix the harissa into the yogurt.

Serve the fritters with a generous spoonful of the harissa yogurt.

GREEN LENTIL LASAGNE

I feel like vegetable lasagne has a bad reputation and is unfairly sidelined. This lasagne is packed full of veg and the creamy ricotta and spinach layer is a speedy and delicious alternative to a traditional béchamel sauce.

SERVES 6

2 tablespoons olive oil

2 red onions, finely chopped

2 garlic cloves, peeled

3 bay leaves

2 × 400g tins chopped tomatoes

2 × 400g tins green lentils, drained and rinsed

450g spinach

500g ricotta

pinch of ground nutmeg

12 lasagne sheets

jar of peppers, drained, rinsed and opened out flat

75g Parmesan or Grana Padano, finely grated

salt and freshly ground black pepper

Preheat the oven to 180°C/gas mark 6. In a large frying pan, heat the olive oil. Add the onions, garlic and bay leaves, then sweat gently for 15 minutes. Fish out the garlic cloves and add the tomatoes and lentils. Bring to the boil, then simmer on a medium heat for 15 minutes. Turn off and fish out the bay leaves.

To make the white layer of the lasagne, wilt the spinach in a saucepan and then press into a sieve to get rid of as much water as possible. Tip into a bowl and mix the spinach with the ricotta and nutmeg. Season and set aside.

To layer up the lasagne, spread a third of the tomato mix into the base of a 20 × 30cm baking dish. Top with a layer of pasta and then a layer of the ricotta mixture, followed by a layer of the peppers. Repeat, ending with the final third of tomato mix.

Cover the top with the grated cheese, then bake in the oven for 35–45 minutes until golden and bubbling. Leave to stand for 5–10 minutes before serving: it'll be easier to cut and handle.

LENTIL LINGUINE WITH CARAWAY CABBAGE

Inspired by delicious buttery cabbage and egg noodles I had in Budapest, this dish is a nod to the flavours of Eastern Europe: sweet and sharp, with a hint of caraway, balanced by the earthiness of lentils.

SERVES 2

25g butter

1 large onion, finely sliced

¼ white cabbage, roughly sliced

1 teaspoon caraway seeds

pinch of caster or granulated sugar

400g tin brown lentils, drained and rinsed

2 teaspoons white wine vinegar

200g linguine (or spaghetti)

2 tablespoons soured cream (or crème fraîche or Greek yogurt), plus extra to serve

salt and freshly ground black pepper

Start by melting the butter gently over a low-medium heat in your largest and deepest frying pan with a lid. When it starts to foam, add the onion, cabbage and caraway seeds, season and then add the sugar, turn the heat to low and fry, covered, for 30 minutes. Check on it now and then to make sure it's not drying out or sticking.

Take the lid off, turn the heat up to medium and continue to cook until the cabbage and onion are starting to turn golden. This should take about 10–15 minutes. Next, add your lentils and vinegar to the pan and continue to cook for 5 minutes.

Boil the pasta in salted water according to pack instructions or until tender, reserve a mug of the cooking water, then drain.

Add the pasta to the frying pan and mix, adding enough of the reserved cooking water to make the sauce coat the pasta. Stir in the soured cream and remove from the heat.

Serve with an extra spoonful of soured cream and some cracked black pepper.

CHICKPEAS, SPICED CARROTS & TAHINI

I like eating this mounded on buttery, herby couscous or alongside a couple of sausages.

SERVES 2

3 carrots, sliced into thick chunks

1½ tablespoons olive oil

1 teaspoon ground cumin

pinch of ground cinnamon

pinch of chilli flakes

2 garlic cloves, finely chopped

400g tin chickpeas, drained and rinsed

1 tablespoon chopped dill

salt and freshly ground black pepper

FOR THE DRESSING

1½ tablespoons olive oil

1 tablespoon tahini

3 tablespoons natural yogurt

juice of 1 lemon

Preheat the oven to 180°C/gas mark 6. On an oven tray, toss the carrots with the olive oil, all the spices and two-thirds of the garlic. Season and roast in the oven for 15 minutes until starting to go a vibrant golden orange colour. At this point, mix in the chickpeas and continue to roast for a further 10 minutes.

Meanwhile, make the dressing. Stir together the olive oil and reserved garlic along with the tahini, yogurt and lemon juice until smooth, then season and set aside until required.

To serve, pile the chickpeas and carrots onto a platter, drizzle with the dressing and sprinkle over the dill.

CANNELLINI BEAN SOUP

This recipe plays on the classic combo of rosemary and garlic. The soft, creamy beans with the warmth of garlic and the heady pine flavour of rosemary work beautifully together. Use organic cannellini beans if possible: they taste better, as does their liquid.

SERVES 4

3 tablespoons olive oil

1 large onion, finely chopped

1 celery stick, finely chopped

4 sprigs of rosemary, leaves chopped

4 garlic cloves, sliced

pinch of chilli flakes

2 × 400g tins cannellini beans (not drained)

½ teaspoon white wine vinegar

salt and freshly ground black pepper

TO SERVE

1 quantity Breadcrumb Topping (page 155) with optional almonds

grated Parmesan (optional)

Heat the olive oil in a large saucepan over a low-medium heat, tip in the onion and celery along with a pinch of salt, and then sweat gently for 10 minutes, stirring often. Add the rosemary, garlic and chilli flakes, then cook for a few further minutes.

Tip in the cannellini beans along with their liquid, then fill the empty tin with water and add this to the pan. Season, bring to the boil and then simmer over a medium heat for 15 minutes.

Stir through the vinegar, then ladle the soup into bowls and top with a generous sprinkling of the breadcrumb mixture and grated Parmesan.

CHICKPEA & SQUASH TAGINE

This dish is perfect for autumnal days when you're feeling in need of a dose of warming spices. If you fancy, try using a mixture of root vegetables or chuck in some aubergine, too.

SERVES 4

2 tablespoons olive oil

2 red onions, thinly sliced

½ teaspoon ground cinnamon

1 teaspoon ground ginger

1 teaspoon ground coriander

1 teaspoon sweet paprika

½ teaspoon ground cumin

2 bay leaves

½ butternut squash, peeled, deseeded and cut into small chunks

2 × 400g tins chickpeas (not drained)

400g tin plum tomatoes

50g dried apricots, roughly chopped

salt and freshly ground black pepper

TO SERVE

couscous or rice

chopped coriander (optional)

Heat the olive oil in a large saucepan, add the onions and sweat gently for 10–15 minutes until turning translucent and tinged golden.

At this point, add all the spices and bay leaves to the onion mixture. Cook for a minute, then add the squash. Toss it in the spices to coat, tip in the chickpeas (along with their liquid), tomatoes and apricots. Top up the pan with enough water to just cover the vegetables, then season. Bring to the boil, then simmer over a low heat for 55–65 minutes until the sauce has thickened a little and the vegetables are tender. Give it a stir now and then to check nothing is sticking and that it hasn't dried out. When serving, carefully remove the bay leaves.

Serve on piles of couscous or rice with a sprinkling of chopped coriander, if you like.

JACKFRUIT & KIDNEY BEAN CHILLI

When jackfruit is cooked, weirdly it shreds just like pulled pork, which gives this chilli a more substantial meatiness. You want to buy young 'green' jackfruit in water for this recipe. Perfect served as part of a Mexican style feast.

SERVES 4

2 tablespoons olive oil

2 onions, finely chopped

2 garlic cloves, finely chopped

1 bay leaf

1 teaspoon ground cumin

1 teaspoon ground cinnamon

1½ teaspoons chilli flakes or powder (ancho or chipotle)

2 × 400g tins chopped tomatoes

400g tin black beans (not drained)

400g tin kidney beans, drained and rinsed

400g tin jackfruit, drained and rinsed

100ml strong coffee

1 teaspoon dried oregano

salt and freshly ground black pepper

Heat the oil in a large saucepan over a medium heat, add the onions, then reduce the heat to low and sweat for 15–20 minutes until soft.

Add the garlic, bay leaf, cumin, cinnamon and chilli flakes and sweat for a further 2–3 minutes. Next, add the tomatoes, black beans (along with their liquid), kidney beans, jackfruit, coffee and oregano, then season. Bring to the boil and then turn down the heat and simmer gently for 45–50 minutes until thickened and the jackfruit is tender. Finally, break up the jackfruit with a wooden spoon until it resembles pulled pork in texture.

Try served with rice or spooned on to corn tortillas with soured cream, guacamole, jalapeños and a cheeky bit of grated Cheddar cheese.

Tip: Make a day ahead to allow the flavours to mingle more, it's made better by waiting.

GREEK BUTTERBEANS

Perfect on toast and covered in feta or topped with a poached egg.

SERVES 2

2 tablespoons olive oil

1 onion, finely chopped

2 garlic cloves, sliced

½ teaspoon ground cinnamon

½ teaspoon chilli flakes (ancho or chipotle)

420g tin butterbeans, drained and rinsed

400g tin chopped tomatoes

1 teaspoon dried oregano

1 tablespoon chopped dill

salt and freshly ground black pepper

Heat the olive oil in a frying pan over a low-medium heat, add the onion, turn to low and gently soften for 10–15 minutes. Add the garlic, cinnamon and chilli flakes and continue to fry for a few minutes.

Add the butterbeans, tomatoes and oregano, then season. Bring to the boil and then simmer gently for 15–20 minutes until thickened a little.

Serve the beans sprinkled with the dill.

BUTTERBEAN, GREEN LENTIL & CHICKPEA STEW

Cooking the onions long and slow creates an amazing depth of flavour.

SERVES 4

2 tablespoons olive oil, plus extra for drizzling

2 onions, finely chopped

2 garlic cloves, sliced

2 bay leaves

1½ teaspoons dried mint

1 teaspoon ground turmeric

400g tin butterbeans, drained and rinsed

400g tin green lentils, drained and rinsed

400g tin chickpeas, drained and rinsed

500ml vegetable stock

200g spinach

salt and freshly ground black pepper

In a large saucepan, heat the olive oil over a low heat. Sweat the onions gently with a pinch of salt until very soft and tinged golden (this will take 30–40 minutes). Then add the garlic, bay leaves, mint and turmeric. Continue to cook for a few minutes until the garlic has softened.

Tip in the butterbeans, lentils and chickpeas along with the stock. Bring to the boil, then turn to a low-medium heat and cook for 20–25 minutes. Add the spinach and allow it to wilt, stirring to incorporate it, then season.

To serve, ladle into bowls and top with an extra drizzle of olive oil. Watch out for the bay leaves when tucking in.

CABBAGE WITH ANCHOVIES & LENTILS

The sweetness of roasted cabbage is a perfect partner to salty anchovies and earthy lentils.

SERVES 2 AS A LIGHT MEAL OR 4 AS A SIDE

1 sweetheart (sometimes called pointed or hispi) cabbage

2 tablespoons olive oil

6 tinned anchovy fillets, drained and finely chopped

3 garlic cloves, sliced

400g tin beluga lentils, drained and rinsed

juice of ½ lemon

2 shallots, finely sliced

a handful of parsley, roughly chopped

salt and freshly ground black pepper

Preheat the oven to 200°C/gas mark 7. Cut the cabbage into about eight wedges and add to a large oven tray.

In a small frying pan, gently heat the olive oil and anchovies, until the anchovies have begun to break down. Add the garlic, fry for about 2–3 minutes, then pour this fragrant oil over the cabbage and season (go easy on the salt, as anchovies are really salty). Toss to combine, add 2 tablespoons of water, then roast for 10–20 minutes until the cabbage is tender and crisp at the edges.

Once the cabbage is cooked, add the lentils to the tray and then roast for a further 2–3 minutes just to warm through.

Meanwhile, put the lemon juice and shallots into a bowl and set aside.

Once the cabbage and lentils are ready, stir through the shallots and parsley. Serve with hunks of bread or on garlic-rubbed toast.

LEEKS, FLAGEOLET BEANS & BLUE CHEESE

This dish works well as part of a spread of salads, as a side for fish or meat, or on its own served over some cheesy, soft polenta. Roquefort, Stilton or Gorgonzola would all work

SERVES 2–3 AS A SIDE

FOR THE DRESSING

1 shallot, finely chopped

1 tablespoon white wine vinegar

1 tablespoon olive oil

½ teaspoon grainy mustard

15g butter

½ tablespoon olive oil

3 large leeks, ends trimmed, cut into thirds horizontally and then cut in half vertically

300ml vegetable stock

400g tin flageolet beans, drained and rinsed

75g blue cheese

salt and freshly ground black pepper

First, start to make the dressing. Put the shallot and vinegar in a bowl or cup and set aside.

To cook the leeks, melt the butter with the olive oil in a deep frying pan, then add the leek slices and brown a little all over. Ensure all the leeks are in a single layer on the base of the pan and then pour in enough stock to come halfway up the leeks (you don't need to use all of the stock). Bring to the boil and then simmer over a low-medium heat for 5–10 minutes until the stock has evaporated and the leeks are tender. Add the flageolet beans and cook for another 2–3 minutes just to warm them.

Once the leeks are cooked and the beans warm, finish making the dressing: add the olive oil and mustard to the shallot and vinegar mixture, season and whisk to combine.

Tip the leeks and flageolet beans on to a large plate or platter, drizzle over the dressing and dot with little pieces of blue cheese.

POTATO & HARICOT HASH

This dish can be mixed up with different leftovers. Swap beets for other root veg, throw in cooked greens or add chorizo, bacon or sausages (if you're that way inclined).

SERVES 4

60g butter

1 onion, coarsely chopped

2 medium boiled potatoes, peeled and coarsely chopped

1 large cooked beetroot, coarsely chopped

400g tin haricot beans, drained and rinsed

4 heaped tablespoons sauerkraut, plus extra to serve

4 eggs

salt and freshly ground black pepper

In a large frying pan, melt half of the butter. Meanwhile, in a bowl, mix the onion, potatoes, beetroot, haricot beans and sauerkraut, then season. Tip into the frying pan, press down firmly and cook over a low-medium heat for 20 minutes until a nice crust forms on the base. Stir and break up the mixture a bit to distribute the crust throughout, then press down again to cook for a further 20 minutes. Repeat once more, this time cooking for 15 minutes over a low heat.

When you're almost ready to serve, melt the remaining butter in another frying pan. When it starts to foam, crack in the eggs, season and fry until the whites have set and the undersides have started to crisp up.

Spoon the hash on to plates and top each portion with a fried egg and extra sauerkraut.

ROASTED CHICKPEAS & SQUASH PASTA

The sweetness and softness of squash works brilliantly with the crisp mild nuttiness of the chickpeas, all wrapped in gloriously warming spices, and served with tart yogurt and a lemony breadcrumb crunch.

SERVES 2 GENEROUSLY

1 small squash or pumpkin, peeled, deseeded and chopped into walnut-sized chunks

½ teaspoon chilli flakes

½ teaspoon fennel seeds

½ teaspoon cumin seeds

generous pinch of ground cinnamon

3 garlic cloves, finely chopped

2 tablespoons olive oil

400g tin chickpeas, drained and rinsed

200g angel hair/vermicelli pasta

2 tablespoons natural yogurt

2 tablespoons chopped parsley

salt and freshly ground black pepper

½ quantity Breadcrumb Topping with optional lemon zest, to serve (page 155)

Preheat your oven to 180°C/gas mark 6.

On a large baking tray, toss together the squash, chilli flakes, fennel and cumin seeds, cinnamon, garlic and oil, then season and roast for 20 minutes, or until the squash is starting to turn golden and soft but still holding its shape.

Toss the chickpeas through and roast in the oven for a further 10 minutes.

Meanwhile, boil the pasta in salted water according to pack instructions or until tender, reserve a mug of the cooking water, then drain.

Using a potato masher, roughly crush about half the butternut squash and chickpea mixture. Add the pasta, yogurt, parsley and enough of the reserved cooking water to the tray to coat the pasta in the sauce. Adjust the seasoning, top with the breadcrumb mixture and serve.

COMFORTING BLACK BEANS

These beans are earthy, salty and smoky. So simple and so delicious. Enjoyed with rice, wrapped in a burrito or fried in a quesadilla, these beans always fit the bill.

SERVES 4

1 tablespoon olive oil

1 large onion, finely chopped

2 garlic cloves, sliced

1 bay leaf

2 teaspoons chilli flakes or powder (ancho or chipotle)

pinch of ground cinnamon

½ teaspoon ground cumin

2 carrots, cut into rounds

2 × 400g tins black beans (not drained)

300ml vegetable stock

salt and freshly ground black pepper

Begin by heating the olive oil in a large frying pan. Add the onion and soften gently for 10 minutes. Then add the garlic, bay leaf, chilli, cinnamon, cumin and carrots and cook for a further 2–3 minutes. Tip in the black beans and stock. Bring to the boil and cook over a medium heat for about 20–25 minutes until the mixture has thickened a little, then season.

Pile into bowls and serve with rice or a dollop of soured cream and some coriander, if you like.

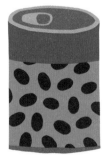

ROASTED COURGETTE & CANNELLINI BEAN DIP

This is quite like hummus and it's delicious eaten warm or cold with soft flatbreads or veg crudités. Za'atar is magic – try sprinkling it on grilled fish, roasted veggies or salads.

SERVES 4

4 courgettes, sliced into chunky rounds

4 tablespoons olive oil, plus extra for drizzling

juice of ½ lemon

2 garlic cloves, crushed

2 tablespoons tahini

400g tin cannellini beans, drained and rinsed

1 teaspoon za'atar spice mix

salt and freshly ground black pepper

Preheat the oven to 220°C/gas mark 9.

Spread the courgettes over two baking trays, drizzle with half the olive oil, season and then roast for 20–25 minutes until golden and tender. The undersides seem to brown much more quickly, so check after about 10–15 minutes and flip if necessary.

Blend two-thirds of the roasted courgettes with the remaining olive oil and the lemon juice, garlic, tahini and cannellini beans until smooth, then season. Tip into a bowl and top with the remaining courgettes. Sprinkle over the za'atar and drizzle with extra olive oil.

BUTTERBEAN, PEPPER & WALNUT SALAD

This is a great dish to make ahead and take for lunch with couscous. If you don't have butterbeans you can use cannellini or haricot beans, instead.

SERVES 2 GENEROUSLY

FOR THE DRESSING

3 red, orange or yellow peppers

75g walnuts

large bunch of parsley, finely chopped

1 garlic clove, finely chopped

5 tablespoons olive oil

1 tablespoon sherry vinegar

200g cherry tomatoes, halved

400g tin butterbeans, drained and rinsed

1 small red onion, sliced as finely as possible

2 tablespoons capers, drained and roughly chopped

salt and freshly ground black pepper

Preheat the oven to 220°C/gas mark 9.

Put the whole peppers on a roasting tray and roast for 30–35 minutes until well blackened, adding the walnuts to the tray for the final 3 minutes of roasting, until a shade darker and smelling fragrant.

Once the peppers are cooked, tip into a bowl and cover with clingfilm (this will make peeling much easier) and set the walnuts aside to cool.

When the peppers are cool enough to handle, peel, deseed and finely chop them. Once the walnuts are cool, finely chop.

In a large bowl, make the dressing: mix the chopped peppers and walnuts with the parsley, garlic, oil and vinegar, then season. Toss with the tomatoes, butterbeans, red onion and capers. Serve on couscous or with garlic-rubbed toast.

CHICKPEA & ONION BHAJIS

These crispy treats are sweet and spicy. Ensure you crush all the chickpeas a little; if you don't they tend to explode when deep-fried. Always be really careful when deep-frying.

MAKES ABOUT 10

100g plain flour

7 tablespoons natural yogurt

2 teaspoons mild curry powder

1 teaspoon ground cumin

1 teaspoon chilli powder

400g tin chickpeas, drained, rinsed and lightly crushed

2 large onions, thinly sliced

2 litres sunflower oil, for frying

salt and freshly ground black pepper

Tip: Try adding 15 thinly sliced fresh curry leaves to the bhaji mixture.

In a large bowl, beat the flour and yogurt together to make a smooth paste. Add the spices, chickpeas and onions, then season.

Add the oil to a large saucepan (it should only come halfway up the side of the pan) and place over a medium-high heat. Line a baking tray with kitchen paper. Wait a few minutes, then test whether the oil is hot enough by dropping a small piece of batter in; if it is hot enough it should sizzle straight away.

When the oil is hot enough, gently drop in heaped dessertspoons of the mixture using a second spoon to scrape it off the first. Fry each for 4–5 minutes, turning halfway through, until golden all over. Remove from the oil using a slotted spoon and place on the paper-lined tray to drain. Repeat until all the mixture is used up. Once finished, turn off the heat and leave the oil to cool fully before cleaning up.

Serve the bhajis with Mango Chutney (page 151).

LENTIL, CHEESE & ONION PUFF PIE

This pie is an appreciation of the cheese and onion pasties of my Devonshire childhood holidays, but this one has the addition of nutty lentils, sweet squash and sneaks in a bit of tangy sauerkraut. Eat while it's hot and the cheese is oozing.

SERVES 6

½ butternut squash, peeled, deseeded and cut into chunks

1 tablespoon olive oil

½ teaspoon chilli flakes

½ teaspoon nigella seeds

50g butter

2 large onions, finely sliced

200ml dry cider

3 tablespoons plain flour

200ml vegetable stock

400g tin beluga lentils, drained and rinsed (you can use the ones in pouches too)

250g mature Cheddar cheese, grated

160g jarred sauerkraut

1 sheet of ready-rolled puff pastry (320g)

1 egg, beaten

salt and freshly ground black pepper

Preheat the oven to 180°C/gas mark 6. You'll need a ceramic or metal dish roughly 30 × 20cm (or a similar-sized circular dish).

Toss the squash with the oil, chilli and nigella seeds, tip onto a baking tray and roast for 20 minutes or until golden and soft but still holding its shape. Set aside.

Meanwhile, melt the butter in a large frying pan, add the onions and a pinch of salt, then fry over a low heat for 20 minutes until soft and tinged golden.

Add the cider, bring to the boil, then rapidly simmer for 2 minutes. Next, add the flour and stir to combine, then simmer for a further 2 minutes. Pour in the stock and boil for a few minutes until thickened. Turn off the heat and add the lentils, cheese, squash mixture and sauerkraut, then season.

Add the filling to your dish and lay the pastry sheet over the top. Press on to the dish edge, trim away any excess, then poke a couple of holes in the lid with a knife and brush with the beaten egg. Place on a baking tray and bake in the oven for 35–40 minutes until well puffed and bubbling.

Tuck in (almost) straight away, while the filling is still fondue-like.

TOMATOES & VEGETABLES

CHERRY TOMATO TOASTS

These are a quick, fresh fix, perfect for brunch or lunch. The delicate creaminess of the ricotta is delicious with the tomatoes and punchy green sauce.

SERVES 2

400g tin cherry tomatoes

2 slices of bread

75g ricotta cheese

salt and freshly ground black pepper

FOR THE GREEN SAUCE

2 tablespoons olive oil

1 garlic clove, finely chopped

handful of basil, leaves picked and finely chopped

3 sprigs of mint, leaves picked and finely chopped

20g Parmesan, grated

1 teaspoon white wine or cider vinegar

Preheat the grill to high.

Tip the cherry tomatoes into an oven tray and grill for 5–10 minutes until starting to blister.

Meanwhile, combine the olive oil with the garlic, herbs, Parmesan and vinegar, season and set aside. Toast the bread, then pop a slice on each plate. Top with the grilled tomatoes and ricotta, spoon over the green sauce and tuck in.

SPICED TOMATO & LENTIL SOUP

Lentil soup has always been a meal of comfort for me; my mum often makes it with her homemade chicken stock, slightly different every time, but it always makes me feel cosy and nourished. It is such an easy and satisfying dish, perfect for a chilly evening.

SERVES 6

1½ tablespoons olive oil, plus extra to drizzle

1 onion, finely chopped

3 garlic cloves, finely chopped

½–1 teaspoon chilli flakes

2 teaspoons ground cumin

2 teaspoons seven spice mix or baharat (or a pinch each of ground cinnamon, cumin, cloves and nutmeg)

350g dried split red lentils

400g tin chopped tomatoes

2 bay leaves

juice of 1 lemon

salt and freshly ground black pepper

Warm the oil in a large saucepan over a low-medium heat, add the onion and cook slowly for about 10–15 minutes until softened. If it begins to brown, turn the heat down. Add the garlic, chilli flakes, cumin and spice mix and fry for a couple of minutes. Add the lentils, tomatoes, bay leaves and 1.85 litres of water. Bring to the boil and then simmer gently until the lentils have swelled and are soft: this should take 25–30 minutes.

When the lentils are tender and breaking down, season, then turn off the heat and add the lemon juice. Spoon the soup (watching out for bay leaves) into bowls and drizzle with a little olive oil.

Tip: Try topping the soup with roasted slices of courgette or carrot: toss in olive oil, salt, pepper and ground cumin and bake in an oven preheated to 200°C/gas mark 7 for 15–20 minutes, or until golden and tender. Or perhaps try topping with a handful of chopped dill, parsley or mint and some crumbled feta.

TURKISH SCRAMBLED EGGS

Digressing from the traditional scrambled eggs situation seemed slightly erroneous, but it was worth it: these are delicious. Serve with toasted pitta for scooping.

SERVES 2

3 tablespoons olive oil

1 onion, finely chopped

1 garlic clove, finely chopped

2–3 fresh jalapeño chillies (or 1 green pepper), deseeded and finely chopped

½ teaspoon chilli flakes

¼ teaspoon hot smoked paprika

½ teaspoon dried oregano

400g tin plum tomatoes, drained and quartered

4 eggs, lightly beaten

salt and freshly ground black pepper

Heat the oil in a frying pan over a low-medium heat, tip in the onion and sweat for 5–10 minutes. Add the garlic, fresh chillies or pepper, chilli flakes, paprika and oregano and cook for a further 5 minutes until the chillies (or pepper) start to soften. At this point, add the tomatoes, season and then simmer for 15 minutes.

Turn the heat to low, then push the tomato mixture to the side of the frying pan. Add the eggs and gently stir until they are just cooked, then fold into the tomato mixture.

Serve with with toasted pitta or with a generous dollop of yogurt.

TOMATOES, GARLIC & GREEN BEANS

My Parisian cousin Sylvie is a great cook. A dish of hers that has stuck in my mind is her roast chicken on a bed of green beans and little tomatoes. This recipe is inspired by it. Serve alongside chicken, with fish or simply with a hunk of bread.

SERVES 2

200g fine green beans, topped, tailed and halved

3 tablespoons olive oil

4 garlic cloves, sliced

2 × 400g tins plum tomatoes, drained

salt and freshly ground black pepper

bread, to serve

In a pan of boiling water, blanch the green beans for 3 minutes, then drain and set aside.

In a large frying pan, heat the olive oil, then add the garlic and fry for a couple of minutes until smelling fragrant and tinged golden. Add the drained tomatoes and green beans, then season. Bring to the boil then reduce the heat and simmer for 10 minutes, covered. Remove the lid and simmer for a further 10 minutes. Delicious hot or cold, and a hunk of bread to soak up all the juices is essential.

SWEETCORN CAKES WITH GREEN CHUTNEY

These sweet and mellow corn cakes go beautifully with the punchy, spicy and tart chutney. This is a perfect brunch dish or light supper.

SERVES 3 GENEROUSLY

FOR THE CHUTNEY

50g coriander, leaves picked

20g mint, leaves picked

1 garlic clove, roughly chopped

juice of ½ lemon

40g desiccated coconut

1 green chilli, finely chopped and seeds left in if you like spice

salt and freshly ground black pepper

FOR THE CORN CAKES

2 × 198g tins sweetcorn (drained and half roughly blitzed)

2 eggs

100g self-raising flour

2 teaspoons mild curry powder

1 small red onion, finely chopped

1 tablespoon flavourless oil (such as sunflower)

1 lemon, quartered (optional)

To make the chutney, put the coriander, mint, garlic, lemon juice, coconut and chilli with 2–3 tablespoons of water into a blender or food-processor. Blitz until smooth, adding more water if needed (the final consistency should be like pesto). Season and set aside.

To make the corn cakes, in a large bowl, mix all the sweetcorn, the eggs, flour, curry powder and onion, then season.

Heat the oil in a large frying pan, then dollop in a heaped tablespoon of mixture for each cake. Flatten each slightly and fry for 3–4 minutes per side until golden and crisp; you may need to do this in batches. Set each batch aside on a plate lined with kitchen paper while you cook the rest.

Serve the cakes with the bright green chutney and garnish with a lemon wedge, if liked.

STICKY POTATOES WITH SPICY TOMATO SAUCE

Patatas bravas meets marinara sauce. The Marsala makes the potatoes sticky and sweet, but it can be swapped out for anything similar you have to hand, stock or water.

SERVES 2

2 large baking potatoes, each cut into about 8 long wedges

2 garlic cloves

2 tablespoons olive oil

2 sprigs of rosemary

100ml Marsala wine (or vegetable stock)

salt and freshly ground black pepper

FOR THE TOMATO SAUCE

1 tablespoon olive oil

1 garlic clove, sliced

1 teaspoon dried oregano

1 teaspoon chilli flakes (use ½ teaspoon if they are extra hot)

400g tin chopped tomatoes

Preheat the oven to 200°C/gas mark 7. On a large oven tray, toss the potatoes with the garlic cloves (bashed with the skin on), the olive oil and the rosemary, then season. Roast in the oven for 30 minutes. Add the Marsala (or stock) and then roast for a further 15 minutes.

Meanwhile, make the sauce: heat the olive oil and add the sliced garlic, oregano and chilli flakes. Cook for 1 minute or so, then add the tomatoes. Season, bring to the boil then cook for 15 minutes on a medium-high heat. Blitz the sauce with a stick blender until smooth (it can be left chunky, if preferred).

Remove the sticky potatoes from the oven and serve straight away with the sauce.

Tip: Try beating 100g of feta into 200ml of soured cream: a cooling antidote to serve alongside the spicy tomato sauce.

BAMBOO SHOOT & AUBERGINE NOODLES

A deliciously creamy, spicy and sweet bowl of salvation.
The texture of aubergine when fried is a thing of beauty;
buttery soft and silky. In this recipe, it's complemented
by the crunch of bamboo shoots.

SERVES 2

FOR THE SATAY SAUCE

2 tablespoons crunchy peanut butter

1–2 tablespoons Chinese chilli oil

2 garlic cloves, finely chopped

2 tablespoons light soy sauce

2.5cm piece of fresh ginger, peeled and
grated (about 1½ tablespoons when grated)

1 tablespoon rice wine vinegar

FOR THE NOODLES

100g flat rice noodles

2 tablespoons flavourless oil (such as
sunflower)

1 aubergine, cut into 2.5cm chunks

**225g tin bamboo shoots, drained and
roughly sliced**

3 spring onions, sliced, whites and greens
separated

Start by mixing everything for the sauce
together along with 150ml warm water,
then set aside.

Boil the noodles for 3 minutes, or according
to the pack instructions, then drain and
refresh under cold water and set aside.

In a wok or large frying pan, heat the oil
over a medium-high heat, then add the
aubergine and fry, stirring often, until
tender and golden (about 5–10 minutes).
Next, add the bamboo shoots and spring
onion whites, fry for a further 2 minutes,
then add the noodles and satay sauce,
stirring to coat.

Pile on to plates and top with the spring
onion greens.

TOMATO, LENTIL & AUBERGINE RAGÙ

When I was growing up, my aunty Sophie often made a big pan of tomatoey lentils when we went round. This version is a nod to a traditional Italian meat ragù, but I have added aubergine instead and served with soft polenta & wilted greens.

SERVES 6

6 tablespoons olive oil

2 onions, finely chopped

2 aubergines, cut into 2.5cm cubes

2 garlic cloves, finely chopped

½ teaspoon fennel seeds

2 bay leaves

pinch of chilli flakes

200ml red wine

2 × 400g tins beluga lentils, drained and rinsed

2 × 400g tins chopped tomatoes

salt and freshly ground black pepper

In a large frying pan, heat 2 tablespoons of the oil, add the onions and soften over a low heat for about 10–15 minutes.

Meanwhile, in another frying pan, heat the remaining oil, add the aubergines and a pinch of salt, then fry on high for 5–10 minutes, stirring often until the aubergine cubes are golden. Set aside.

By this point, the onions should be soft and tinged golden. Add the garlic, fennel seeds, bay leaves and chilli flakes. Fry for a further 2–3 minutes, then tip in the wine. Bring to the boil and boil until it has reduced by two-thirds in volume (this shouldn't take more than 5 minutes). Last but not least, add the lentils, tomatoes and the browned aubergine cubes. Season and reduce the heat, then simmer for 15–20 minutes until the sauce has thickened a little and the aubergine is buttery soft.

Just before serving, fish out the bay leaves. This ragù is great with soft polenta, pasta or served simply with a hunk of bread.

FLAGEOLET BEAN & ARTICHOKE GRATIN

If you don't eat fish the anchovies can be left out. If you do eat fish, don't be tempted to leave them out anyway just because you think you don't like them; they bring a subtly salty depth to this rich and creamy dish.

SERVES 2

25g butter

2 onions, chopped

3 garlic cloves, sliced

3 sprigs of rosemary, finely chopped

3 tinned anchovy fillets, drained and finely chopped

50g soft, fresh breadcrumbs

30g Parmesan, grated

400g tin flageolet beans, drained and rinsed

400g tin artichoke hearts in water, drained, rinsed and torn in half

200ml double cream

salt and freshly ground black pepper

Tip: Experiment with adding a pinch of chilli flakes when you're softening the onion.

Preheat the oven to 180°C/gas mark 6. Melt the butter in a frying pan over a low-medium heat. Once the butter is foaming, add the onions, garlic, rosemary and anchovy fillets. Turn to low and soften gently for 20–25 minutes until the onions are tender and turning golden.

Meanwhile, mix the breadcrumbs with the Parmesan and set aside.

Once the onions have softened, add the beans and artichoke hearts, season and heat through for 5–6 minutes, then add the cream. Bring the mixture almost to the boil, then tip into a baking dish and top with the cheesy breadcrumbs. Bake for 25–30 minutes until golden and bubbling. Serve with a hunk of crusty bread and some salad.

A CLASSIC
TOMATO SOUP

I felt like it was a must to include this recipe in this book. Of course, a ready-made tin of tomato soup has its place but this soup has more depth and freshness, and it's almost as easy to make.

SERVES 2

2 tablespoons olive oil

1 onion, finely chopped

1 celery stick, finely chopped

1 carrot, diced

1 garlic clove, finely chopped

1 teaspoon dried oregano

400g tin chopped tomatoes

pinch of sugar

½ teaspoon red wine vinegar

2 tablespoons crème fraîche

salt and freshly ground black pepper

a handful of basil, roughly chopped, to serve

In a large saucepan, heat the olive oil, then add the onion, celery, carrot and garlic and soften gently for 10–15 minutes. Tip in the oregano, tomatoes, sugar and 300ml of water and season. Bring to the boil, then turn down and simmer for 20 minutes until thickened a little.

Either blitz smooth with a stick blender or simply pass over with a potato masher for a chunkier soup. Stir in the vinegar.

Ladle into bowls, then swirl the crème fraîche into each and top with some basil.

INDIAN EGGS WITH TOMATOES

These eggs are simply flavoured with sweetness from the tomatoes and coconut. This is a perfect breakfast served up with some chapatis and a good dollop of yogurt.

SERVES 2

1 tablespoon desiccated coconut

1 tablespoon flavourless oil (such as sunflower)

½ teaspoon brown mustard seeds

1 shallot (or ½ onion), finely chopped

1 green chilli, deseeded and finely chopped

10 fresh or dried curry leaves

¼ teaspoon ground turmeric

400g tin plum tomatoes, drained and rinsed

4 eggs, beaten and seasoned

salt and freshly ground black pepper

In a cup, cover the coconut with boiling water, then set aside.

Heat the oil in a medium-sized frying pan over a high heat, then add the mustard seeds. When they start to pop, which will be about 30 seconds, add the shallot and green chilli, then reduce the heat to medium and fry for 3–5 minutes until just starting to colour.

Add the curry leaves and turmeric, then fry for a further 30 seconds. Add the tomatoes and soaked coconut, along with its liquid and roughly break each tomato into two or three pieces. Bring to the boil and simmer for 5–10 minutes over a medium heat until most of the liquid has evaporated. Season.

Scoop the tomato mixture into a bowl and set aside. Drip a little more oil into the pan, turn the heat to medium-high. Tip in the eggs and allow them to set, pulling back the edges to allow any raw egg to fill the gaps. Cook until golden on the base and still damp on top. Dollop the tomato mixture evenly on top of the eggs. Cook for 30 seconds more then fold in half and cut in two and serve. Try serving with Quick Chapatis (see page 146), Mango Chutney (see page 151) and natural yogurt, if liked.

ARTICHOKE CARBONARA

Carbonara is such a quick supper. It is rich and creamy (without any cream) thanks to the egg yolks and mountains of cheese. Artichokes bring a slight citrus flavour that balances the richness of the sauce.

SERVES 2

2 tablespoons olive oil

2 onions, finely chopped

1 large egg, plus 2 yolks

pinch of ground nutmeg

50g Parmesan, finely grated, plus extra to serve

2 garlic cloves, sliced

400g tin artichoke hearts, drained, rinsed and roughly torn

200g spaghetti

salt and freshly ground black pepper

Heat the olive oil in a large frying pan over a medium heat. Once hot, add the onion, turn the heat down and sweat gently for 20 minutes.

Meanwhile, beat together the egg, extra yolks, nutmeg and cheese, then season (be generous with the black pepper) and set aside.

Add the garlic to the pan and fry for 1 minute. Next, add the artichokes, cover with a lid and heat gently while you cook the spaghetti.

Boil the spaghetti in a pan of salted water according to the pack instructions or until tender, scoop out a mug of cooking water, then drain.

Remove the frying pan from the heat and immediately tip in the spaghetti. Toss in the sauce and then pour in the egg and cheese mixture. Working quickly, toss the pasta in the mixture, taking care to not allow the eggs to sit on the base of the pan (they may scramble). Once the pasta is coated, add a little of the reserved cooking water, if needed, to create a glossy sauce.

Mound on to plates and top with extra Parmesan and black pepper.

TOMATO, CHICKPEA & OKRA MASALA

I love curry. I am a slight addict and have recently come to the conclusion that most things are improved when curried.

SERVES 2

2½ tablespoons flavourless oil (such as sunflower)

1 teaspoon brown or black mustard seeds

1 teaspoon fenugreek seeds

1 large onion, thinly sliced

2.5cm piece of fresh ginger, peeled and finely grated

3 garlic cloves, finely chopped

3 teaspoons garam masala

400g tin chickpeas (not drained)

400g tin plum tomatoes

500g okra (ladies' fingers), trimmed and sliced into 3cm pieces

salt and freshly ground black pepper

Heat 1½ tablespoons of the oil in a deep frying pan. Once hot, add the mustard seeds, wait until they start to pop (about 30 seconds) and then add the fenugreek seeds. Shortly after, add the onion and a pinch of salt, turn the heat down and sweat for 10–15 minutes until the onion is soft and turning golden.

Add the ginger, garlic and 2 teaspoons of the garam masala and cook for a further 3–4 minutes. Add the tin of chickpeas, including their liquid, and the tomatoes. Season and cook for 20 minutes, or until the tomatoes have broken down and the curry has thickened a little.

Meanwhile, in a separate frying pan, heat the remaining oil and garam masala, then fry the okra pieces for 6–7 minutes until nicely browned. Set aside.

Once the curry has thickened, add in the okra and cook for a further 5–6 minutes. Serve steaming bowls of curry alongside flatbread (try the Quick Chapatis on page 146), yogurt or Coconut Rice (see page 147).

LAYERED TOMATOES, COURGETTES & POTATOES

Aubergine would work well here instead of the courgette, as would a torn ball of mozzarella added alongside the Parmesan.

SERVES 4

3 courgettes, sliced into thick rounds

650g potatoes, peeled and cut into 1cm-thick slices

5 tablespoons good-quality olive oil

2 garlic cloves, thinly sliced

2 × 400g tins plum tomatoes

1 teaspoon dried oregano

25g basil, leaves picked and chopped

25g parsley, leaves picked and chopped

60g Parmesan, grated

50g fresh breadcrumbs

15g butter

salt and freshly ground black pepper

Place the sliced courgettes in a colander. Sprinkle with ½ teaspoon of salt, toss so all the slices are coated and leave to drip over the sink for 30 minutes.

Preheat the oven to 180°C/gas mark 6. Bring a large saucepan of salted water to the boil and boil the potatoes until the outer edges are just tender (start checking after 2 minutes). Drain and tip into a large roasting tin. Drizzle over 2 tablespoons of the olive oil, season and roast in the oven for 25–35 minutes until soft and turning golden.

Once the courgettes have finished draining, tip them into a second, deep roasting tin or ovenproof dish, toss with 2 tablespoons of the olive oil and roast in the oven alongside the potatoes for 25–30 minutes until golden.

Meanwhile, heat the remaining tablespoon of oil in a large frying pan, add the garlic and fry for a few minutes until just turning golden. Add the tomatoes and oregano, then season. Bring to the boil and then turn down and simmer for 20 minutes. Stir through the basil and parsley and set aside.

Once the courgette slices are cooked, top them with half the tomato sauce followed by half the cheese and then all of the roasted potato slices. Spread the remaining tomato sauce over the top, sprinkle with the breadcrumbs and remaining cheese, then dot with the butter. Bake for 20 minutes until golden and bubbling.

SWEETCORN CHOWDER

This soup is a lovely soft yellow; it sings with the colour of spring and gently soothes.

SERVES 4

FOR THE SOUP

1 tablespoon butter

1 tablespoon olive oil

small bunch of spring onions, sliced

1 bay leaf

1 potato (approx. 280g), peeled and cut into small chunks

400ml milk

400ml vegetable stock

3 × 198g tins sweetcorn, drained

FOR THE CROÛTONS

2 slices of bread

1 tablespoon olive oil

70g cheddar cheese, coarsely grated

salt and freshly ground black pepper

Preheat the oven to 200°C/gas mark 7. In a large saucepan, melt the butter with the olive oil over a low-medium heat. When it starts to foam, add the spring onions and bay leaf. Sweat for 4–5 minutes until they begin to soften.

Stir in the potato, then add the milk and stock. Bring just to the boil, then simmer for 10–12 minutes until the potato is tender. Add the sweetcorn and cook for a further 2 minutes to just warm it through. Discard the bay leaf. Blitz the soup until smooth using a blender. If it's too thick, let it down with a little milk or water to your desired consistency.

Meanwhile, for the croûtons, tear the bread into smallish chunks, add to a baking tray along with the olive oil, season and bake in the oven for 10 minutes until turning golden. Sprinkle over the cheese and return to the oven for a few minutes until the cheese is oozy and bubbling.

Ladle the soup into bowls and top with the cheesy croûtons.

Tip: Try adding a little cayenne pepper or chilli flakes to the soup for a warming kick.

WATER CHESTNUT & SHIITAKE DONBURI

This dish is inspired by the yasai katsudon I often ate with my neighbours when I was growing up. Our gardens were joined, so we were always nipping in and out. This dish reminds me of them.

SERVES 2

35g butter

1 onion, sliced

120g fresh shiitake mushrooms, thickly sliced

225g tin sliced water chestnuts, drained and roughly chopped

1 tablespoon grated (peeled) fresh ginger

1 tablespoon Marsala

3 tablespoons soy sauce

200ml fish stock

4 eggs, beaten

150g jasmine rice, cooked according to pack instructions

Melt the butter in a small frying pan over a medium heat, then add the onion, mushrooms and water chestnuts. Fry, stirring often until the onion is softening and the mushrooms and water chestnuts are turning golden, about 5–10 minutes, then add the ginger and cook for a further 2 minutes.

Add the Marsala, soy sauce and fish stock. Bring to the boil and then reduce the heat to a simmer. Tip in the eggs, swirl in a little, then cover and simmer for 1 minute. When you take the lid off, the eggs should remain a bit runny on top.

Divide the cooked rice between two bowls and top with the vegetable and egg mixture.

Tip: If you don't have jasmine rice, use basmati or long grain instead.

CORN, CHARD & CHEESE TART

This is a great dish to prep ahead for a picnic or to make at the start of the week to cut up and take into work for lunch.

SERVES 6

1 quantity simple shortcrust pastry (see page 150) or a 500g block ready made shortcrust pastry

FOR THE FILLING

50g butter

2 onions, thinly sliced

pinch of sumac

1–2 teaspoons chilli flakes

8 sprigs of lemon thyme, leaves picked and chopped

200g Swiss chard, thinly sliced

340g tin sweetcorn, drained and half blitzed with a stick blender

200ml crème fraîche

3 eggs

100g feta, crumbled

salt and freshly ground black pepper

salad, to serve

Tip: To blind bake; line the pastry case with greaseproof paper, then fill with uncooked rice and bake for 20 minutes. Remove the rice and paper and cook for a further 10 mintes until lightly golden.

Preheat the oven to 180°C/gas mark 6. You'll need a loose-bottomed 25cm tart tin.

To make the filling, melt the butter in a large frying pan over a medium heat, then add the onions with a pinch of salt, sumac and half the chilli flakes and lemon thyme. Turn the heat to low, then soften slowly for 30–35 minutes, until sticky and golden. Next, add the chard and cook for a further 4–5 minutes until it is wilted and any excess moisture has evaporated. Season and remove from the heat.

In a bowl, beat together the sweetcorn, crème fraîche and eggs, season and then set aside. In a separate bowl, toss the feta with the remaining chilli flakes and lemon thyme.

Roll the pastry out so that it is about 5cm larger than your tart tin. Carefully drape the pastry into the tin, lightly pressing into the base and sides of the tin, then trim off the excess and generously prick the base with a fork. Chill in the fridge for 20 minutes. Heat a baking tray in the oven.

Blind bake (see tip) and then reduce the temperature to 160°C/gas mark 4.

Tip the onion mixture into the case, spread evenly across the base, then pour in the egg mixture. Scatter over the feta mixture and bake in the oven for 25–30 minutes until just set in the middle and golden on top.

Allow to cool slightly before removing from the tin. Slice up and serve with a salad.

FISH

CRAB THORAN

I first had a crab thoran at a small Indian restaurant near where I grew up in South East London, and it still remains one of my favourite dishes. The combination of the sweet crab and coconut with the earthy mustard seeds and the warmth from the ginger and chilli is really delicious.

SERVES 2 AS A STARTER OR SMALL LUNCH

2 tablespoons flavourless oil (such as sunflower)

½ tablespoon brown or black mustard seeds

1 teaspoon fenugreek seeds

2 shallots, finely chopped

½ tablespoon grated (peeled) fresh ginger

1 green chilli, finely chopped

20 fresh or dried curry leaves

2 tomatoes, chopped and deseeded

5 tablespoons desiccated coconut, steeped in boiling water for 10 minutes

2 × 170g tins lump crab meat, drained

1 lime, cut into wedges, to serve

Heat the oil in a frying pan over a high heat, then add the mustard seeds. Wait until they start to pop (about 30 seconds) and then add the fenugreek seeds. Fry very briefly until fragrant. Reduce the heat to low and add the shallots, ginger and chilli. Fry, stirring often, for a further 5–10 minutes, or until the shallots are softening and golden.

Add the curry leaves, tomatoes and coconut (along with the soaking liquid). Cook for a few minutes until the tomatoes are starting to break down, then carefully stir through the crab meat and serve, garnished with a lime wedge.

This dish goes well with the Quick Chapatis on page 146 or Coconut Rice on page 147.

HERBY TUNA & HARICOT BEAN SALAD

This salad is super simple, it's delicious served straight away but also works really well the next day for lunch.

SERVES 2

FOR THE DRESSING

1 teaspoon Dijon mustard

2 teaspoons vinegar (white wine or cider)

1 tablespoon olive oil

zest of 1 lemon

1 shallot, finely chopped

15g dill, leaves picked and finely chopped

160g tin tuna in olive oil, drained

410g tin haricot beans, drained and rinsed

1 small cucumber, deseeded and cut into half moons

salt and freshly ground black pepper

bread or toast, to serve

Start by making the dressing: whisk the mustard, vinegar and oil together. Season and then stir in the lemon zest, shallot and dill.

In a separate bowl, mix the tuna, beans and cucumber together, then pour over the dressing and toss lightly to combine. This is best served with a slice of bread or toast to mop up all the juices.

SALMON FISHCAKES WITH SAUERKRAUT

When I was little I used to go for lunch at family friend Ruth's. I have fond memories of her little salmon fishcakes; to my 5-year-old mind there were mountains of them. I felt such anticipation as the plate was passed through the kitchen hatch.

SERVES 4

2 × 170g tins skinless and boneless red or pink salmon, drained

400g floury potatoes (Maris Pipers are great), boiled, cooled and roughly mashed

2 shallots (or ½ onion), finely chopped

1 teaspoon caraway seeds

zest of 1 lemon (then lemon sliced into wedges to serve)

plain flour, for dusting

2 teaspoons flavourless oil (such as sunflower), plus more if needed

40g salted butter

4 heaped tablespoons jarred sauerkraut

4 tablespoons soured cream

salt and freshly ground black pepper

Tips:
Try sprinkling the finished dish with some chopped dill or parsley.

You can flavour these in a multitude of ways: try adding some thinly sliced lime leaf and finely chopped chilli and serve with lime wedges. For an Indian twist, mix in some ground turmeric and cumin and thinly sliced curry leaf, then serve with a dollop of yogurt or Mango Chutney (see page 151).

Mix together the salmon, potatoes, shallots (or onion), ½ teaspoon of the caraway seeds and the lemon zest, then season. Shape into eight small patties. Chill the fishcakes in the fridge for 20 minutes to firm up.

Just before cooking, dust the tops and bottoms of the fishcakes in a little flour. Heat the oil in a frying pan over a medium heat, then add the fishcakes. Cook for 6–7 minutes per side until golden, then roll the sides across the pan briefly to brown, too.

Melt the butter in a separate small frying pan. When it starts to foam, add the remaining caraway seeds. Fry briefly until the butter smells nutty and is beginning to brown.

To serve, divide the fishcakes between four plates and top with the sauerkraut and soured cream. Drizzle over a little of the fragrant butter, and liberally squeeze with the lemon wedges at the table.

ANCHOVY PASTA WITH STICKY ONIONS

Tinned anchovies are magic, they can be melted into a multitude of things to create an extra depth of salty complexity, which they do here in this comforting pasta dish.

SERVES 4

1 tablespoon olive oil

35g butter

3 onions, finely sliced

2 garlic cloves, finely chopped

50g tin anchovy fillets, drained and finely chopped

150ml milk

400g spaghetti

a handful of parsley, chopped

salt and freshly ground black pepper

Tip: Try with the Breadcrumb Topping on page 155.

Add the olive oil and butter to a large frying pan over a medium heat. Tip in the onions and garlic, turn the heat to low and sweat slowly for 20–25 minutes until soft and golden, stirring often.

Once the onions have turned golden, add the anchovies. Allow them to melt away into the onion mixture, then stir in the milk, season and continue to cook for about 5–10 minutes. Once the onion mixture has started to break down, remove from the heat and roughly mash.

Meanwhile, boil the pasta in a pan of salted water according to the pack instructions until tender, reserve a mug of the cooking water, then drain.

Tip the pasta straight into the sauce along with most of the parsley and enough of the reserved cooking water to make the sauce coat the pasta, tossing to mix. Divide between four plates and sprinkle with the remaining parsley.

SMOKED MACKEREL PÂTÉ & QUICK PICKLES

This quick and simple pâté is perfect as a starter or can be boxed up and taken for lunch. Try adding a little finely chopped shallot or onion to the quick pickles for added punch.

SERVES 2

FOR THE QUICK PICKLES

½ large cucumber, sliced into rounds

1 teaspoon salt

2 tablespoons white wine vinegar

½ teaspoon coriander seeds, lightly crushed

½ teaspoon fennel seeds, lightly crushed

2 tablespoons caster sugar

FOR THE PÂTÉ

2 × 110g tins smoked mackerel fillets in oil, drained

100g crème fraîche

juice of ½ lemon

½ teaspoon fennel seeds, lightly crushed

sea salt and freshly ground black pepper

toast, to serve

Start by making the quick pickles: place the cucumber in a sieve and sprinkle with the salt. Leave to stand over the sink (or a bowl) for 20 minutes. Squeeze to get rid of any excess moisture and pat dry.

Meanwhile, in a bowl, mix together the vinegar, coriander and fennel seeds and the sugar, stirring until the sugar has dissolved. Submerge the cucumber slices. They can be eaten straight away, or will keep, covered, in the fridge for a few days.

To make the pâté, mash the mackerel fillets with the crème fraîche, lemon juice and fennel seeds. Season and enjoy spread on toast topped with the quick pickles.

A SRI LANKAN MACKEREL CURRY

I went to Sri Lanka nearly ten years ago, but the flavours of the food have stayed with me. I often revisit my notebook with the recipes I scribbled down while watching people cook there. This recipe draws on those flavours.

SERVES 4

3 × 125g tins mackerel in sunflower oil, drained and 2 tablespoons oil reserved

1 teaspoon brown or black mustard seeds

1 teaspoon fenugreek seeds

3 cardamom pods, bashed

1 onion, finely sliced

1 tablespoon grated (peeled) fresh ginger

5 garlic cloves, finely chopped

1 red chilli, finely chopped and seeds left in for more heat, if liked

15–20 fresh or dried curry leaves

2 × 400g tins plum tomatoes

100ml coconut milk

salt and freshly ground black pepper

rice or chapatis, to serve

Heat the reserved mackerel oil in a saucepan over a high heat, then add the mustard seeds. When they start to pop (about 30 seconds) add the fenugreek seeds and cardamom pods. Fry briefly until fragrant, then reduce the heat to low-medium and add the onion with a pinch of salt. Sweat the mixture gently for 10–15 minutes until soft and tinged golden.

Add the ginger, garlic, chilli and curry leaves, then fry for 1–2 minutes. Add the tomatoes and season. Bring to the boil, then simmer over a medium heat for 15 minutes until thickened slightly.

Gently add the mackerel, taking care to keep the pieces whole, reduce the heat to low and cook for 10 minutes to warm the mackerel through. Just before serving, stir in the coconut milk. Serve alongside rice or Quick Chapatis (see page 146).

CRAB FRIED RICE

Crab is something a bit special, often expensive and a bit off limits, not to mention fiddly. Tinned crab is delicious and a fraction of the price of fresh. I often make fried rice: it's a great vehicle for pretty much anything! If you live near a Chinese supermarket, explore all the different chilli oils available. Laoganma Black Bean Chilli Sauce is a personal favourite.

SERVES 4

1 tablespoon flavourless oil, such as sunflower

200g green beans, cut into 3cm pieces

4 garlic cloves, finely chopped

200g jasmine rice, cooked and cooled (or use any leftover rice)

1 teaspoon chilli oil, plus extra to serve

2 tablespoons soy sauce

small bunch of spring onions, sliced and whites and greens separated

2 eggs, beaten

2 × 170g tins lump crab meat, drained

2 teaspoons toasted sesame oil

Tip: Feel free to leave the eggs out or try frying four eggs in a little oil to top the rice instead.

In a large frying pan or wok, heat the groundnut or sunflower oil over a medium heat. Once hot, add the green beans. Fry for 3–4 minutes until starting to colour, then add the garlic, rice, chilli oil, soy sauce and spring onion whites. Fry, stirring often, until the rice has heated through, about 3–4 minutes.

Push the rice mixture to one side of the pan and pour the beaten eggs into the space. Allow the eggs to begin to set, then pull the sides into the middle, ensuring all the egg comes into contact with the pan. Once it is all cooked, use a spatula to break it into pieces and stir into the rice mixture. Turn off the heat and stir through the crab meat and sesame oil.

Pile into bowls and top with the sliced spring onion greens and an extra drop of chilli oil, if you fancy.

POTATO LATKES WITH SALMON PÂTÉ

Latkes are a thing of my childhood, one of two things (the other being doughnuts) that made Hanukkah vaguely interesting to me as a small child. Here they are served alongside a twist on the classic soured cream. I like to have a few pickles to nibble on, too.

SERVES 2 (MAKES ABOUT 8)

FOR THE LATKES

1 onion, coarsely grated

500g potatoes, peeled and coarsely grated

1 egg

½ tablespoon plain flour

3 tablespoons flavourless oil (such as sunflower)

FOR THE PÂTÉ

170g tin skinless and boneless red or pink salmon, drained

4 tablespoons soured cream

1 teaspoon finely chopped tarragon

zest of 1 lemon, plus 1 teaspoon juice

salt and freshly ground black pepper

gherkins, to serve

Put the grated onion and potatoes in a clean tea towel, then squeeze out as much liquid as you can. Tip the potato and onion into a large bowl, add the egg and flour, season and then mix everything together. Set aside.

To make the salmon pâté, in a small bowl, mix together the salmon, soured cream, tarragon and lemon zest and juice, then season and set aside.

When you're ready to cook your latkes, heat the oil in a large frying pan over a medium heat. Once hot, drop in heaped tablespoons of the potato mixture and flatten each slightly with a spatula. Fry for a few minutes per side until golden and crisp (you may need to cook them in batches). Drain on kitchen paper and then transfer to a plate or rack while you finish cooking the remaining latkes.

To serve, divide the latkes between plates and top with the salmon pâté and a few gherkins, if you like.

CRAB LINGUINE WITH CHERRY TOMATOES

Cherry tomatoes and crab are a great combination. Using pre-peeled cherry tomatoes is preferable, as the skins can be a bit tough. The sweetness is married with the heady aniseed flavour of fennel, the tang from the lemon and a tingle of warmth from the chilli.

SERVES 2

1 tablespoon olive oil

2 garlic cloves, sliced

pinch of chilli flakes

pinch of fennel seeds

400g tin peeled cherry tomatoes, drained

200g linguine

170g tin lump crab meat, drained

zest and juice of ½ lemon

a handful of basil, leaves picked and thinly sliced

salt and freshly ground black pepper

Heat the oil in a large frying pan over a medium heat, then add the garlic, chilli flakes and fennel seeds. Fry for a few minutes until the garlic is smelling fragrant and tinged golden. Add the tomatoes, season and continue to cook for 10 minutes until thickened a little but with the tomatoes still holding some shape.

Meanwhile, boil the linguine in a pan of salted water according to the pack instructions or until tender, reserve a mug of the cooking water, then drain.

Add the linguine and crab to the sauce, gently fold together and finish by adding the lemon zest and juice with enough of the reserved cooking water to make the sauce coat the pasta.

Pile the pasta on to two plates and serve with a scattering of basil, if you like.

SMOKED MACKEREL KEDGEREE

My granny always made a very decadent kedgeree for brunch gatherings when I was growing up. The sweet and mildly spiced rice is sumptuous with the smoky fish.

SERVES 4

300g basmati rice, rinsed

20g butter

2 × 110g tins smoked mackerel in oil, drained and 2 tablespoons oil reserved, broken into large chunks

2 onions, chopped

1 green chilli, finely chopped and deseeded

4 cardamom pods, bashed

2 bay leaves

1 tablespoon mild curry powder

3 eggs, boiled to your preference, peeled and quartered

salt

1 lemon, cut into wedges, to serve

Tip: Try scattering with fresh coriander and a spoonful of yogurt.

Boil the rice in plenty of boiling, salted water according to pack instructions, drain and rinse under cold running water, then set aside.

In a large frying pan, melt the butter with the reserved mackerel oil over a low-medium heat. Add the onions, chilli, cardamom pods and bay leaves, turn the heat to low and soften gently for 15 minutes.

Add the curry powder and cook for a further 30 seconds. Stir in the rice to warm through, then add the fish chunks and gently toss together, taking care not to break up the fish too much. Top with the eggs and serve with the lemon wedges.

Watch out for the cardamom pods and bay leaves when eating.

SICILIAN SARDINES ON TOAST

Taking inspiration from the flavours of Sicily and the very British dish of Welsh rarebit, this speedy supper was born.

SERVES 2

2 × 120g tins sardines in oil, drained

1 egg yolk

zest of 1 lemon (and then cut lemon into wedges)

pinch of chilli flakes

pinch of fennel seeds

35g pine nuts, toasted and chopped

35g sultanas, chopped

130g ricotta cheese

4 slices of bread

salt and freshly ground black pepper

Preheat your grill to high.

In a large bowl, using a fork, mash the sardines with the egg yolk, lemon zest, chilli flakes, fennel seeds, pine nuts, sultanas and ricotta, then season. Lightly toast your bread and then spread with the sardine mixture. Place on a baking tray and grill until a golden crust forms. Serve with the lemon wedges.

Tip: Try adding fennel: very finely slice a fennel bulb, toss with a little olive oil and lemon juice, season and place on top of the toast when it comes out from under the grill.

SARDINE & LEMON LINGUINE

I am a total sardine convert. In this recipe, the rich and oily sardines are balanced with sweet onion, sharp lemon and the crunch of warm, garlicky breadcrumbs. I challenge you to make this even if you think you hate fishy fish!

SERVES 2

1 tablespoon olive oil

120g tin sardines in olive oil, drained and oil reserved

1 onion, finely sliced

2 garlic cloves, finely sliced

pinch of chilli flakes

sprig of rosemary

200g linguine (or spaghetti)

zest and juice of 1 lemon

½ quantity Breadcrumb Topping (page 155)

salt

Heat the olive oil and the reserved oil from the sardines in a heavy-based frying pan over a medium heat, then add the onion, garlic, chilli flakes and rosemary. Turn the heat to low and fry slowly until sweet, sticky and golden (this should take about 15–20 minutes).

When the onion is nearly done, boil the pasta in a pan of salted water according to the pack instructions or until tender, reserve a mug of the cooking water, then drain.

Tip the pasta into the sauce, then mash in the sardines and add the lemon zest and juice along with enough of the reserved cooking water to make the sauce coat the pasta.

Mound the pasta on to plates and liberally sprinkle with the golden breadcrumbs.

VIETNAMESE CRAB CAKES

These are inspired by a Vietnamese dish of fish marinated in lots of turmeric, ginger and garlic, pan-fried and served with the classic Vietnamese dressing Nước cham. I've repurposed these flavours into crisp crab cakes.

SERVES 2

FOR THE CRAB CAKES

2 × 170g tins lump crab meat, drained

2.5cm piece of fresh ginger, peeled and grated (about 1½ tablespoons when grated)

1 red chilli, deseeded and finely chopped

1 garlic clove, finely chopped

15g dill, finely chopped

1 teaspoon ground turmeric

2 shallots, finely chopped

10 tablespoons dried breadcrumbs

2 eggs, beaten

1 tablespoon flavourless oil (such as sunflower)

FOR THE DRESSING

4 teaspoons fish sauce

juice of 1 lime

4 teaspoons soft brown sugar

1 red chilli, deseeded and finely chopped

1 garlic clove, finely chopped

To make the crab cakes, mix the crab, ginger, chilli, garlic, dill, turmeric, shallots, 4 tablespoons of the breadcrumbs and half the beaten eggs in a bowl. Shape into eight patties and stick in the fridge to firm up for at least 20 minutes.

To make the dressing, mix all the ingredients with 2 tablespoons of water, check the balance of sour, sweet and salty and adjust accordingly.

Just before frying, dip each cake in the remaining beaten egg and then into the remaining breadcrumbs to coat. Heat the oil in a large frying pan over a medium heat and fry the cakes for 4 minutes per side until golden.

Serve alongside the dressing, for drizzling or dunking.

Tip: Try nestling a crab cake in a lettuce leaf with some finely sliced cucumber, then drizzle with the dressing.

ANCHOVY MAC 'N' CHEESE

Mac 'n' cheese is a classic and a favourite of mine. It's taken to another level here with the addition of salty anchovies, sweet onion and bay leaves.

SERVES 4

50g butter

7 tinned anchovy fillets, drained and finely chopped

1 onion, finely chopped

3 bay leaves

350g macaroni

50g plain flour

650ml whole milk

350g mature Cheddar cheese, grated

75g fresh breadcrumbs (from about 2 slices)

1 large tomato, sliced

salt

Worcestershire sauce, to serve

Tip: Try subbing out some of the macaroni pasta for blanched cauliflower florets for something a little lighter.

Preheat the oven to 200°C/gas mark 7.

To make the sauce, melt the butter with the anchovies in a frying pan over a low heat, then add the onion and bay leaves and cook gently for about 20–25 minutes until the onion is very soft.

Meanwhile, boil the pasta in a pan of salted water according to pack instructions or until tender, then drain and rinse under cold water. Set aside.

Once the onion is soft, stir in the flour and continue to cook for 2 minutes. Next, add the milk, a little at a time, stirring to incorporate before adding more. Cook, stirring often, until the sauce has thickened a little. Remove from the heat and melt in two-thirds of the cheese. Carefully remove the bay leaves. Mix the remaining cheese with the breadcrumbs.

Tip the pasta into an ovenproof dish (roughly 30 x 20cm), then pour the sauce over and mix to combine. Top with the breadcrumb/cheese mixture and sliced tomato. Bake for 25–35 minutes until golden and bubbling vigorously.

Serve with lashings of Worcestershire sauce.

TUNA, TOMATOES & GNOCCHI

This dish is very quick to make, satisfying and delicious. If you can't find or don't fancy gnocchi, it can be substituted for cooked dried pasta such as penne.

SERVES 4

2 tablespoons olive oil

1 red onion, finely chopped

½ teaspoon chilli flakes

pinch of ground cinnamon

2 × 400g tins of chopped tomatoes

2 tablespoons capers, drained

2 × 160g tins of tuna in oil, drained

500g fresh gnocchi

zest and juice of ½ lemon

250g mozzarella, drained and roughly torn

salt and freshly ground black pepper

Tips:
This recipe is extra yummy with a pinch of fennel seeds added along with the chilli flakes. If you don't have capers, pitted olives would also work really well. You could throw in some chopped basil or parsley, too.

If you don't have mozzarella, top with grated Parmesan or Cheddar instead.

Preheat the oven to 200°C/gas mark 7.

Heat the oil in a frying pan over a medium heat, then add the onion, chilli flakes and cinnamon. Turn the heat to low and sweat for 10–15 minutes or until soft and beginning to turn golden. Add the tomatoes, capers and tuna, and season. Bring to the boil and then simmer over a medium heat for 20 minutes.

Meanwhile, boil your gnocchi in a pan of salted water for 1 minute, then drain.

Tip the gnocchi into the sauce, then add the lemon zest and juice. Transfer everything into a baking dish and top with the mozzarella, then bake for 20 minutes until golden and bubbling.

ROASTED POTATO & TUNA NIÇOISE

A classic salad niçoise centres around tomatoes, anchovies, olives and olive oil, with other additions being at the whim of the maker. So, this is my perfect niçoise.

SERVES 4

700g small new potatoes, large ones halved

6 tablespoons olive oil

200g fine green beans, halved

2 tablespoons capers, drained

6 tinned anchovy fillets, drained and finely chopped

1 tablespoon Dijon mustard

1 garlic clove, finely chopped

2 tablespoons white wine vinegar

2 Little Gem lettuces, leaves separated and large ones sliced

2 ×160g tins tuna in olive oil, drained and flaked

a handful of basil leaves, thinly sliced

3 tablespoons finely chopped chives

salt and freshly ground black pepper

Preheat the oven to 180°C/gas mark 6.

Toss the potatoes in a baking tray with 2 tablespoons of the oil and a splash of water, season and roast for 30–40 minutes, or until golden and tender.

Meanwhile, boil the beans for about 5 minutes, until just tender, then drain and refresh under cold water. To make the dressing, mix together the capers, anchovy fillets, mustard, garlic, vinegar and the remaining olive oil, then season.

Mix the warm potatoes with the dressing and then tip into a serving dish. Toss with the lettuce, green beans and tuna, then sprinkle over the herbs.

Serve straight away to avoid the lettuce wilting. This dish does work really well as a packed lunch, too: keep the lettuce separate until you're about to eat.

TUNA AND FLAGEOLET BEAN PASTA

The sweetness of the slowly cooked garlic in partnership with the warmth of the chilli melds perfectly with the delicate flageolet beans and tuna.

SERVES 4

2 tablespoons olive oil

2 garlic cloves, finely sliced

1 red chilli, finely chopped and deseeded

400g spaghetti or linguine

400g tin flageolet beans, drained and rinsed

2 × 160g tins tuna in olive oil, drained

bunch of parsley, chopped

zest and juice of ½ lemon, plus extra to serve

salt and freshly ground black pepper

Heat the olive oil in a large frying pan over a low heat, then stir in the garlic and chilli and fry very gently until the garlic is soft and lightly golden, about 5–10 minutes.

Meanwhile, boil the pasta in a pan of salted water according to pack instructions or until tender. Reserve a mug of the cooking water, then drain.

Add the beans to the frying pan, increase the heat to medium and warm through for 4–5 minutes. Add the drained pasta, tuna, parsley and lemon zest and juice with enough of the reserved cooking water to coat the pasta in the sauce. Season generously with black pepper and toss to combine. Serve piled high with an extra squeeze of lemon.

SKIPPERS WITH SWEET AND SOUR BEETROOT

Cooking beetroot in this way is so quick; the sweetness of the butter offsets its earthiness perfectly. You could try topping the skipper-laden toast with a poached egg to make this into a more substantial dinner.

SERVES 2 AS A LIGHT DINNER OR LUNCH

25g butter

1 teaspoon caraway seeds

2 large raw beetroot, peeled and coarsely grated

2 large gherkins, sliced, plus 2 tablespoons of the pickling liquid

2 thick slices of bread

106g tin skippers in oil, drained and flaked

2 tablespoons soured cream

salt and freshly ground black pepper

Melt the butter in a frying pan over a medium-high heat. When it's foaming, add the caraway seeds and cook for 30 seconds.

Next, add the grated beetroot and fry for 3 minutes. Add the gherkin pickling liquid and cook for a further 1 minute, then season and turn off the heat.

Toast the bread, then top with the beetroot, flaked skippers and sliced gherkins. Serve soured cream alongside.

MACKEREL TACOS

My citrus-laden salsa and the spicy soured cream are best friends with the smoky mackerel. These are fun, quick and easy to rustle up, perfect for sharing with friends and a cold beer.

SERVES 4

½ small red cabbage, thinly sliced

1 teaspoon fine salt

2 ripe avocados, peeled, destoned and sliced

8 small corn tortillas

3 × 110g tins smoked mackerel fillets in oil, drained and flaked into large chunks

freshly ground black pepper

FOR THE SALSA

4 tomatoes, deseeded and roughly chopped

1 small red onion, finely chopped

large bunch of coriander, roughly chopped

juice of 2 limes

FOR THE SPICY SOURED CREAM

8 tablespoons soured cream

2 tablespoons hot sauce (or more if you like heat)

Put the cabbage into a colander and sprinkle over the salt. Rub it all over the cabbage and leave to drain over the sink for 20 minutes.

To make the salsa, put the tomatoes in a bowl and mix in the onion, coriander and half the lime juice, then season with black pepper and set aside. In another bowl, mix the soured cream with the hot sauce to make your spicy soured cream. Toss the avocado with the remaining lime juice.

Squeeze any excess moisture out of the cabbage, then tip into a clean bowl.

Heat a large griddle or frying pan, then cook the tortillas for 30 seconds or so per side until warm and with brown spots. Stick the stack of warm tortillas on the table with the bowls of spicy soured cream, salsa, cabbage, avocado and the flaked mackerel, layer up and tuck in.

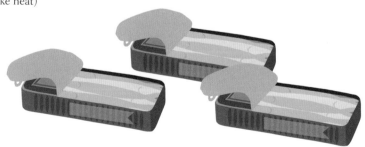

APPLE, FENNEL & CRAB SALAD

This salad is light, crisp, sweet and sharp, with a spicy kick from the chilli and ginger. It makes a lovely light supper for summer evenings.

SERVES 2

FOR THE DRESSING

1 teaspoon grated (peeled) fresh ginger

1 shallot, finely chopped

1 tablespoon cider vinegar

1 tablespoon olive oil

1 red chilli, deseeded and finely chopped

salt and freshly ground black pepper

1 fennel bulb, very thinly sliced

1 pink grapefruit, peeled and segmented

1 Granny Smith apple, quartered, cored and thinly sliced

170g tin lump crab meat, drained

To make the dressing, mix together the ginger, shallot, vinegar, olive oil and chilli, then season.

Tip the fennel, grapefruit and apple into a large bowl, add the dressing and toss to coat.

Divide between two plates and top each with some crab.

FRUIT &
SWEET TINS

PEAR & YOGURT PANCAKES

Delicious fluffy pancakes are a great brekkie. I like adding frozen raspberries or blackberries to the pears and drizzling everything with a crazy amount of maple syrup.

SERVES 4 (MAKES ABOUT 12 PANCAKES)

320ml yogurt, plus extra to serve

2 eggs

200g plain flour

1 teaspoon bicarbonate of soda

pinch of ground cinnamon

1 teaspoon sugar

410g tin pears in juice, sliced into wedges and juice reserved

juice of 1 lemon

pinch of ground nutmeg

1 tablespoon butter, plus extra for frying

salt

To make the pancakes, combine the yogurt and eggs in a jug. In a large bowl, mix the flour, bicarbonate of soda, cinnamon, a pinch of salt and half the sugar, then whisk in the contents of the jug to make a smooth batter.

In a small saucepan, add the pears and the reserved juice with the lemon juice, remaining sugar and the nutmeg. Bring to the boil and cook for about 5 minutes until the pears are soft and the liquid has largely evaporated. Stir in the butter, then set aside.

Melt a little butter in a large frying pan over a medium heat, then dollop in a heaped tablespoon of the batter for each pancake and cook for 2–3 minutes per side until golden and springy. You will most likely need to do this in batches.

To serve, divide the pancakes between four plates and top with the pear compote and a little extra yogurt, if you like.

MANGO & CARDAMOM LASSI

Cool, sweet and fruity; this lassi is a perfect partner to a curry or anything else spicy. You can also have it for brekkie topped with granola and fruit.

SERVES 2

200ml yogurt

200ml tinned mango purée (or equivalent of tinned mango slices)

a small handful of ice cubes (about 6 or so)

2 cardamom pods, seeds removed and crushed

Stick all your ingredients in a blender and whizz until smooth. Pour into glasses and enjoy straight away.

Tip: This lassi is thick, so if you want a thinner drink, simply stir in a little cold water or milk.

PEACH & RASPBERRY LAYERED PUDDING

This falls somewhere between a trifle and a tiramisu and both in my view are delicious. Try playing with the fruit, booze and cake to shape this to your preferences.

SERVES 6

300g tin raspberries in syrup

zest and juice of ½ lemon

1 drop rosewater (optional)

3½ tablespoons caster sugar

415g tin peach slices, drained

small plain sponge cake (about 250g)

6 tablespoons sweet alcohol (cassis, Chambord, fruit brandy or Marsala all work well)

250g mascarpone

1 large egg, separated

250ml double cream

salt

In a saucepan, mix together the raspberries (and their syrup), lemon juice, rosewater, if using, 1½ tablespoons of the sugar and a small pinch of salt. Place over a medium heat for about 5 minutes to thicken a little, then stir in the peach slices. Leave to cool while you prepare the rest of the pudding.

Cut the sponge into flat 1cm slices (as if you're cutting a loaf of bread) and lay in a large bowl or dish. Douse in the sweet alcohol and allow it to soak in thoroughly. In a bowl, beat the mascarpone with the remaining sugar and the egg yolk until smooth. In another bowl, whisk the egg white to stiff peaks, then fold that into the mascarpone. Finally, in a third bowl, whip the cream to soft peaks and then fold it into the mascarpone mixture.

Top the soaked sponge with the fruit from the pan and then carefully spoon over the mascarpone mixture (you want to try to avoid knocking all of the air out of it) and spread into an evenish layer. Cover and refrigerate for 1 hour or so before tucking in. To serve, top with the lemon zest.

PRUNE & GINGER MUFFINS

This recipe is for my dad who loves ginger cake. These muffins are gloriously sticky and perfect for a weekend breakfast, either spread with butter or served cold with a cup of tea.

MAKES 12

100g golden syrup

100g black treacle

100g slightly salted butter

70g dark muscovado sugar

175g self-raising flour

½ teaspoon baking powder

2 teaspoons ground ginger

1 teaspoon ground cinnamon

2 eggs, beaten

50ml milk

60g walnuts, roughly chopped

290g tin prunes, drained and chopped

Preheat the oven to 160°C/gas mark 4 and line a 12-hole muffin tray with cases.

Put the golden syrup, black treacle and butter in a saucepan over a low heat and melt them together. Add the sugar and continue to heat for 1 minute, then set aside to cool a little.

Mix the flour, baking powder and spices in a large bowl. Pour in the contents of the saucepan followed by the eggs, milk, walnuts and prunes and stir briefly to mix.

Divide the mixture between the muffin cases and bake for 25–30 minutes until well risen and they spring back up when pressed gently. Allow to cool briefly in the tray before tucking in or popping on to a wire rack to cool fully; they'll keep in an airtight container for up to 5 days.

FIG & ORANGE BLOSSOM FOOL

This very simple pudding is inspired by the sticky baklava I get from the Turkish shop at the end of my road: rich, floral and thoroughly addictive.

SERVES 4

150ml double cream

100g Greek yogurt

1 drop orange blossom water (or the zest of ½ orange, or both)

425g tin figs in syrup, drained and 2 tablespoons syrup reserved, figs roughly chopped

2 tablespoons toasted unsalted pistachios, roughly chopped

zest of ½ orange (optional)

In a bowl, whip the cream to soft peaks, then gently fold in the yogurt, orange blossom water, figs and reserved syrup.

Divide the mixture between four tumblers or ramekins and top with the pistachios just before serving. Sprinkle over a little extra orange zest, if you like.

Tip: If you can't get hold of figs, use tinned prunes in syrup instead.

NO-CHURN RICE PUDDING ICE CREAM

Rice pudding is one of my all-time favourites. Give me any excuse to make or eat it and I will. Here it's transformed into an Indian-inspired ice cream, bringing back memories of my trip to Rajasthan, where drinking ginger-heavy tea was the start to every day.

SERVES 8

600ml double cream

1 cinnamon stick

7 black peppercorns

3 cardamom pods

½ teaspoon fennel seeds

25g fresh ginger (about 2.5cm piece), peeled and sliced

400g tin rice pudding

8 tablespoons condensed milk

1 tablespoon rum or brandy

Tip: Try adding chopped almonds or pistachios to your mixture, or a tea bag at the infusing stage to make chai tea ice cream.

Put the cream into a heavy-based saucepan with all the spices. Bring to just below the boil, stirring regularly, then turn off the heat, cover and leave to cool and infuse.

Once cooled, refrigerate until fully cold (if it isn't it won't whip, so make sure it is fridge-cold). Strain into a bowl and whip into soft peaks, then gently fold in the rice pudding, condensed milk and rum or brandy. Transfer to a covered container and freeze for at least 4–6 hours. Take out of the freezer and pop into the fridge to soften slowly for 40 minutes before serving.

PEAR & PRUNE COBBLER

Sweet and sticky with a hit of fiery ginger, this is just the ticket for chillier days, doused in a healthy amount of cream.

SERVES 6–8

3 × 411g tins pears in juice, drained and cut into quarters

290g tin prunes in juice (not drained)

6 pieces stem ginger in syrup, finely chopped

juice of 1 lemon

100g soft brown sugar

125g slightly salted cold butter, cut into small cubes

250g self-raising flour

50g almonds (or pecans or hazelnuts), roughly chopped

cream or ice cream, to serve

Preheat the oven to 170°C/gas mark 5.

In a baking dish (roughly 1.5 litres in capacity) mix the pears, prunes (and their juice), stem ginger, lemon juice and 50g of the sugar. Bake in the oven for 10 minutes.

Meanwhile, to make the topping, in a large bowl, rub the butter into the flour until it resembles fine breadcrumbs. Stir in the remaining sugar and the nuts. Add 2–3 tablespoons cold water and using your hands bring together into a dough.

Remove the fruit from the oven. Using your hands, roll the dough into small balls, then sit them on top of the fruit, leaving space in between each ball. Return to the oven for 25–30 minutes until the topping is golden and puffed up and the fruit below is bubbling. Tuck in straight away with scoops of ice cream or a river of cream.

BANOFFEE PIE WITH HAZELNUT CREAM

What is not to love about sweet banana, buttery biscuits and a load of nutty, chocolate cream? I feel my Granny Susan, who ate bananas with double cream and a sprinkling of caster sugar, would agree.

SERVES 8

FOR THE CASE

325g digestive biscuits

200g slightly salted butter, melted

100g blanched hazelnuts, toasted and finely chopped

FOR THE CARAMEL FILLING

125g golden caster sugar

397g tin condensed milk

125g slightly salted butter, cut into small pieces

FOR THE TOP

3–4 bananas

squeeze of lemon juice

300ml double cream

3 tablespoons Nutella

Begin with the case: in a food-processor, blitz the digestives until you have fine crumbs (alternatively, put into a freezer bag and whack with a rolling pin). Tip into a bowl with the melted butter and 75g of the chopped hazelnuts, and mix to combine. Press the mixture into a 26cm loose-based tart tin, then pop in the fridge while you make the filling.

For the filling: add the sugar to a large, non-stick frying pan, put over a low-medium heat and allow to melt: do not stir! Once melted, turn up the heat and simmer hard until it has turned a deep, golden colour. Turn the heat to low and slowly stir in the condensed milk. It may not come together immediately; keep stirring and it will become smooth and uniform in colour, about 10 minutes. Add the butter, stirring until melted and combined. Pour into your chilled case, smooth the surface and put back into the fridge for at least 1 hour.

When you're ready to serve, peel and slice the bananas, toss with a little lemon juice (this will stop them going brown) and lay over the caramel. Whip the cream to soft peaks, fold in the Nutella, then spread over the bananas. Sprinkle over the reserved hazelnuts to serve.

Tip: If you've got time to spare and prefer a less labour intensive approach, an alternative method for the caramel layer is to place the unopened tin of condensed milk in a saucepan. Cover with boiling water, then simmer over a low heat, uncovered (checking the water level remains at least 2.5cm above the tin) for about 3 hours. Allow to cool completely before opening and tipping the contents into the prepared case.

ROCKY ROAD WITH FIGS & WALNUTS

Rocky road's traditional marshmallow stickiness has been replaced by tinned figs in this recipe. Sweet and juicy, they work perfectly with the rich dark chocolate and almondy crunch of amaretti biscuits.

MAKES 10 BARS

170g slightly salted butter, diced

335g dark chocolate, broken into squares

4 tablespoons golden syrup

120g walnuts, toasted and roughly chopped

120g amaretti biscuits, broken into small pieces (digestives, lotus or hobnobs would also work well)

425g tin figs in syrup, drained and chopped

Line a 20cm square brownie tin with greaseproof paper.

In a medium saucepan, slowly melt together the butter, chocolate and golden syrup, then fold in most of the walnuts, biscuits and figs. Tip into the prepared tin, spreading evenly, and top with the remaining ingredients. Chill in the fridge to firm up (about 2–3 hours minimum) before cutting into ten bars.

COCONUT MILK SET CREAM

I love panna cotta, it's such a simple and delicious pudding. This coconut set cream is a tropical variety, served up with juicy, sweet pineapple. Yum.

SERVES 4–5

4 premium grade gelatine leaves

400ml double cream

400ml tin coconut milk

160g soft brown sugar

zest and juice of 2 limes

435g tin pineapple slices, drained

20g unsalted butter, plus extra for greasing moulds

salt

Grease four or five small glasses or dariole moulds. Soak the gelatine in cold water for 5 minutes.

In a small saucepan, heat the cream and coconut milk with 120g of the sugar, a pinch of salt, the lime zest and half the lime juice. Heat, stirring often, until the sugar has dissolved. Remove from the heat, squeeze any excess water out of the gelatine and add to the cream, stirring until fully dissolved.

Pour the mixture into the glasses and put in the fridge to set for at least 4 hours.

When you're ready to serve, sprinkle the remaining 40g of sugar over the pineapple slices. Warm a large, non-stick frying pan over a medium heat, add the butter, then the pineapple, and cook on both sides until the pineapple is golden and sticky. Transfer to a plate and squeeze over the remaining lime juice.

To turn out the coconut creams, dip the glasses or moulds into hot water briefly and then invert each on to a plate. Serve each with a slice of caramelised pineapple.

CHOCOLATE & CHERRY POTS

Dark, rich and decadent, these little pots are the perfect prep-ahead pud.

SERVES 4

425g tin pitted cherries in syrup, roughly chopped and syrup reserved

juice of 1 lemon

2 tablespoons soft light brown sugar

2 egg yolks

150g dark chocolate, cut into small pieces

170ml double cream

2 cardamom pods, bashed

salt

In a small frying pan, heat the cherries, syrup, lemon juice and half the sugar until thickened. Divide the cherries between four glasses and refrigerate until needed.

Put the egg yolks and remaining sugar in a bowl with a pinch of salt. Whisk until pale and increased in volume and then set aside. Put the chocolate into a heatproof bowl and set aside.

In a small saucepan, heat the cream with the cardamom pods, stirring until it just comes to the boil.

Pour the hot cream through a sieve over the chopped chocolate. Leave to stand for 1 minute (to allow the chocolate to melt), then stir vigorously to amalgamate (it should come together and be glossy). Immediately pour the chocolate mixture over the egg yolk mixture, whisking constantly until combined.

Spoon the chocolate mixture over the cherry layer in the glasses, allow to cool, then refrigerate for at least 2 hours or until it's time to eat.

PINEAPPLE, LIME & COCONUT CAKE

This kitsch cake has lost its cherries and gained the duo of coconut and lime. It's perfect served with a big scoop of rum 'n' raisin ice cream.

SERVES 10

For the pineapple layer

100g caster sugar

40g unsalted butter

435g tin pineapple rings in juice, drained

FOR THE SPONGE

200g unsalted butter, softened, plus extra for greasing

200g soft light brown sugar, plus 1 tablespoon

4 eggs

zest and juice of 2 limes

200g self-raising flour

50g desiccated coconut

ice cream or cream, to serve

Preheat your oven to 160°C/gas mark 4. Grease a 23cm cake tin (not loose-bottomed) with butter.

For the pineapple layer, put the caster sugar, along with 2 tablespoons of water, in a small saucepan over a low heat to dissolve the sugar. Bring to the boil and cook (without stirring) until it has turned a deep caramel colour. Add the butter and swirl to incorporate. Pour into the prepared cake tin to create an even layer on the base, then set aside to cool for a few minutes. Place the pineapple rings on top of it.

To make the sponge, beat the butter and 200g sugar together until light and fluffy. Beat in the eggs, one at a time, followed by the lime zest, then fold in the flour and coconut. Carefully spoon the mixture over the pineapple and spread out so it's even. Bake in the oven for 35 minutes until risen and golden. Meanwhile, mix the lime juice with the extra sugar and 1 tablespoon of water. Set aside.

Once the cake comes out, leave it to stand for 5 minutes, then turn out on to a plate and drizzle over the lime juice mixture; enjoy warm with a scoop of ice cream.

SPICED PUMPKIN & CHOCOLATE BREAD

A delicious and easy recipe that uses tinned pumpkin, perfect for breakfast or teatime. Add a simple cream cheese icing, scattered with extra chopped pecans to turn it into more of a showstopper.

SERVES 8–10

125g softened unsalted butter, plus extra for greasing

175g caster sugar

2 eggs

½ teaspoon vanilla extract

250g self-raising flour (white, wholemeal or half and half)

½ teaspoon ground nutmeg

1 teaspoon ground cinnamon

250g tinned pumpkin purée

75g dark chocolate, chopped

75g pecans, chopped (or another nut of your choosing or dried fruit)

salt

Preheat your oven to 160°C/gas mark 4. Grease a large loaf tin with butter and line with greaseproof paper.

In a bowl, beat the butter and sugar together until pale and fluffy. Beat in the eggs, one at a time, then the vanilla. Fold in the flour, spices, a pinch of salt and the pumpkin purée, followed by the chopped chocolate and pecans.

Pour into the prepared tin and bake for about 60–70 minutes, until a skewer poked into the centre comes out clean. Leave to cool in the tin before turning out and diving in!

Tip: The spices can be changed or some left out; try using ground mixed spice, cloves, baharat mix, ginger or the zest of an orange.

CHERRY PIE

It is really worth making your own pastry. Buttery and melt-in-the-mouth, it isn't too tricky and doesn't take long. Try it.

SERVES 8

FOR THE PASTRY

155g cold butter, cut into small cubes

285g plain flour, plus extra for rolling

pinch of salt

40g icing sugar

2 egg yolks, plus 1 egg, beaten, for brushing

FOR THE FILLING

2 × 425g tins pitted cherries in syrup, drained

2 tablespoons cornflour

zest and juice of 1 lemon

340g cherry conserve

ice cream or cream, to serve

You will need a roughly 24cm pie tin. To make the pastry, rub the butter into the flour, salt and icing sugar until it resembles damp sand. Add the egg yolks and 1–2 tablespoons of very cold water. Using the rounded side of a butter knife, cut into the mixture until it starts coming together. When it starts to form large clumps, bring together into a ball with your hands. Flatten into a disc, wrap in clingfilm and chill in the fridge for 30 minutes (to ensure it's well chilled before you start rolling).

Meanwhile, to make the filling, combine all the ingredients in a large bowl.

Preheat the oven to 180°C/gas mark 6 and pop a baking tray in the oven to heat up while you build your pie. Remove your pastry from the fridge and cut off two thirds. Lightly dust the work surface with flour. Roll this into a circle slightly larger than your pie tin, lower into the tin and gently press into the base and up the sides. Leave any overhang and brush the lip with a little of the beaten egg.

Roll the remaining pastry into another circle large enough to form the lid. Spoon the filling into the tin, then press your second circle on to the egg-brushed overhang, squeezing together. Trim the two layers of pastry using scissors about 1cm away from the edge of your tin, then crimp in any way you choose (lots of help on YouTube). Brush the top with the beaten egg and poke a couple of holes into the lid.

Put the pie in the oven on the hot tray and bake for 30–40 minutes until golden. Leave to cool for about 30 minutes in the tin, then serve with a scoop of ice cream or lashings of cream.

PEACH, MANGO & PASSION FRUIT PAVLOVA

This impressive pud, given a little time and care, isn't too tricky to pull off. I like to make it a day ahead and leave it cooling in my oven overnight, ready to be dressed the next day. If you're new to meringues, I urge you to give this a go.

SERVES 6–8

5 egg whites (very carefully separated to avoid any yolk contamination)

325g caster sugar

1½ teaspoons cornflour

1½ teaspoons white wine vinegar

zest of 2 limes and juice of 1

425g tin peach slices, drained

425g tin mango slices, drained

250ml double cream

200ml Greek yogurt

4 passion fruits, seeds scraped out

salt

Tips: Try crushing cardamom seeds and adding them to the peach and mango mixture. Save all the egg yolks in the fridge for an extra indulgent omelette or scrambled egg weekend breakfast.

Preheat the oven to 100°C/gas mark ½ and line a large baking tray with greaseproof paper. Draw a circle on the paper using a plate about 22cm in diameter, then flip the paper so the line is on the underside.

In a large bowl, slowly whisk the egg whites with a pinch of salt using an electric whisk on medium speed until peaks start forming. Gradually, 1 tablespoon at a time, beat in the sugar (ensuring it is fully incorporated and dissolved before adding more). Continue whisking until the mixture is stiff and glossy and there is little to no graininess remaining. Mix the cornflour and vinegar together, then fold in until just combined.

Scoop the meringue mixture onto the lined tray and spread out to form a large circle, building the sides up a little so they are higher than the middle. Put into the oven and bake for 1 hour, then turn the oven off, leaving the pavlova inside to cool fully.

While you wait, put the lime zest and juice in a bowl with the peach and mango slices and a little pinch of salt.

When you're ready to assemble, whip the cream to soft peaks, fold in the yogurt and carefully dollop over the top of the cooled pavlova. Adorn with the peach mixture and passion fruit seeds. Serve straight away.

CREATIVE
CUPBOARD
ACCOMPANIMENTS

QUICK CHAPATIS

These are the easiest form of bread I've come across (except possibly going to buy some). Give them a go; they take minutes and only four ingredients.

MAKES 4 (ABOUT THE SIZE OF A SIDE PLATE)

200g plain wholemeal or white flour (or ideally half and half)

1½ tablespoons flavourless oil (such as sunflower)

1 teaspoon black onion seeds (optional)

salt

Tip: To make coconut roti, soak 100g of desiccated coconut in 150ml boiling water for 10 minutes, add to 200g plain flour and 30g melted butter, pinch of salt and 1 teaspoon black onion seeds, knead, rest and cook as above.

In a large bowl, mix together the flour, a generous pinch of salt, the oil and the black onion seeds. Gradually add just enough warm water to make a soft, pliable dough, it should be about 125–150ml. Knead for 5–10 minutes until you have an elastic dough; the longer you knead, the softer it will be.

Place the dough back in the bowl and cover with a tea towel, then rest for at least 20 minutes.

When you're ready to cook the bread, divide the dough into four, and shape each into a ball (ensuring to cover the dough you're not currently working on), then flatten the dough until it's the size of a side plate (about 20cm). You can do this either by using a rolling pin or by pressing the dough in between your palms, working outwards, stretching occasionally.

Place a frying pan over a high heat. Once it's really hot, add one chapati and cook for about 30 seconds per side (there should be dark brown welts on each side, and it may puff up if your pan is really hot). Repeat the process with all four. Eat immediately.

COCONUT RICE

Coconut rice I could eat on its own by the pan load, slightly sweet yet salty with a thoroughly savoury note from the fenugreek.

SERVES 4

400g basmati rice

1 tablespoon flavourless oil (such as sunflower)

1 onion, finely chopped

2 garlic cloves, sliced

1 teaspoon fenugreek seeds

400ml tin coconut milk

salt

Wash the rice until the water runs clear, then put it in a bowl and cover with cold water. Set aside for 30 minutes.

Meanwhile, heat the oil in a medium-sized, lidded saucepan, then add the onion, garlic and fenugreek seeds. Sweat for 10 minutes over a low-medium heat until the onion is soft and sticky.

Once the rice has soaked, drain and stir into the onion mixture along with a pinch of salt, the coconut milk and 350ml of water. Bring to the boil, then cover and immediately turn the heat to low. Cook for 7 minutes, turn off the heat and set aside for 5 minutes, then take the lid off and fluff up the rice using a fork. It's great served with the Tomato, Chickpea & Okra Masala on page 66 or the Crab Thoran on page 79.

Tip: Try adding about 10–12 curry leaves along with the fenugreek seeds.

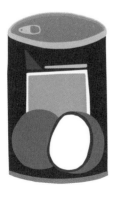

OATY SODA BREAD

This bread is sweet, salty and rich. It's best eaten the same day it's made, but is still yummy toasted and slathered in butter for a few days after. If you can't get buttermilk, this can be made using natural yogurt.

MAKES 1 LOAF

165g plain white flour

165g plain wholemeal flour

1 teaspoon fine salt

1½ teaspoons bicarbonate of soda

50g rolled oats

1 teaspoon sugar

300ml buttermilk

2½ tablespoons black treacle

Tips:
If you can't get through a whole loaf, slice up and freeze so you have it ready to go straight into the toaster.

Try adding a handful of sultanas or raisins and some roughly chopped walnuts to the dry ingredients.

Preheat the oven to 180°C/gas mark 6. Mix together all the dry ingredients in a large bowl.

Once the oven has reached temperature, make a well in the centre of your dry mixture and pour in the buttermilk and treacle. Using a wooden spoon, mix until you have a soft, sticky dough.

Using floured hands, shape the dough into a round, then pop on to a lightly floured baking tray. Using a sharp knife, cut a deep cross about one-third of the way through the dough and dust with flour. Bake for 45–50 minutes until the loaf sounds hollow when tapped underneath.

Leave to cool on a wire rack before tucking in. Try spreading the treacle butter overleaf for a decadent snack.

TREACLE BUTTER

This was conceived midway through testing a cake recipe. The slightly savoury and metallic treacle with salty butter and a little sugar makes for a splendid spread; try it on warm soda bread.

SERVES 4

80g slightly salted butter, softened

2½ tablespoons soft light brown sugar

3 tablespoons black treacle

Beat the butter with the sugar until really soft, then slowly beat in the treacle until well combined. Eat slathered over warm Oaty Soda Bread (see page 148) or with Pear Pancakes (see page 114).

SHORTCRUST PASTRY

This buttery pastry is perfect for tarts, pies and quiches. If you don't need the whole amount it can be easily frozen for a couple of months, then defrosted overnight in the fridge when you need it next.

MAKES ENOUGH TO LINE A 25CM TART TIN

155g very cold butter, diced

285g plain flour

good pinch of salt

2 egg yolks

To make the pastry, rub the butter into the flour and salt until it resembles damp sand. Add the egg yolks and 1–2 tablespoons of very cold water. Using the rounded side of a butter knife, cut into the mixture until it starts coming together When it starts to form large clumps, bring together into a ball with your hands. Flatten into a disc, wrap in cling film and chill in the fridge for 30 minutes before using.

MANGO CHUTNEY

To be honest, I was pretty astonished that mango chutney can be made (and made deliciously) from tinned mango. Ditch the fluorescent orange chutney from the shops; this is worth making.

MAKES 1 JAR APPROX. 350ML

2 × 425g tins mango slices in juice, drained and chopped into small chunks

1 teaspoon chilli flakes

30g fresh ginger (about 4cm piece), peeled and grated

4 garlic cloves, finely chopped

180g soft light brown sugar

250ml white wine or cider vinegar

1 teaspoon black onion seeds

Add everything to a saucepan, bring to the boil, then turn down to a simmer for about 40–50 minutes until thick and jammy, ensuring to stir occasionally to check it's not catching on the bottom. Scoop into a hot, sterilised jar. Allow to cool slightly, then seal. Once open, store it in the fridge; it should keep for a few months.

Tip: Try popping a layer of it under some Cheddar for your next cheese on toast. It's the best.

FIG & RED ONION JAM

This is the perfect partner for cheese, ham, pâté or cooked meats.

MAKES 1 JAR, APPROX. 500ML

3 tablespoons olive oil

500g red onions, finely sliced

75g soft brown sugar

425g tin figs, roughly chopped, syrup reserved

2 bay leaves

1 star anise

150ml red wine vinegar

70ml Marsala (or red wine)

salt and freshly ground black pepper

Heat the oil in a large frying pan over a low-medium heat. Add the onions along with a pinch of salt and fry gently for about 30 minutes until they are very soft.

Next add 2 tablespoons of the sugar, with the figs, bay leaves and star anise, then continue to cook for 10 minutes. Add the vinegar and Marsala (or red wine) and remaining sugar, then season. Bring to the boil, then turn down to a simmer for about 30–40 minutes until the mixture becomes sticky and jam-like. Keep your eye on it, in case it sticks or dries out.

Scoop into a hot, sterilised jar. Allow to cool slightly, then seal. Once open, store it in the fridge; it should keep for a few months.

A KICK-ASS ANCHOVY DRESSING

This dressing is great for leafy salads, boiled tatties or green veggies (roasted, boiled or steamed), or even tossed through pasta with a tin of tuna thrown in. Easy-peasy dinners.

MAKES APPROX. 150ML

1 shallot, finely chopped

1 tablespoon vinegar (white wine or cider)

50g tin anchovy fillets, drained and finely chopped

1 teaspoon Dijon mustard

1 garlic clove, very finely chopped

½ teaspoon chilli flakes

75ml your nicest olive oil

1 tablespoon chopped oregano, basil or parsley (optional)

salt and freshly ground black pepper

In a bowl, mix the shallot and vinegar together, then set aside for 5 minutes.

Add the anchovies, mustard, garlic and chilli flakes to the shallot. Gradually beat in the olive oil, check and adjust the seasoning and add any herbs, if using. It'll keep well in a sealed jar or an airtight container in the fridge for about a week.

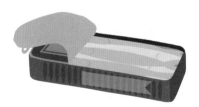

BREADCRUMB TOPPING

A versatile, crunchy addition to many dishes.
Great for adding some extra texture and a boost
of flavour. Try experimenting with chilli flakes,
caraway, fennel or cumin seeds, chopped nuts
or other citrus zest.

SERVES 4

2 tablespoons olive oil

1 garlic clove, finely chopped

100g fresh breadcrumbs (see Tip)

35g blanched almonds, roughly chopped
(optional)

zest of 1 lemon (optional)

In a frying pan, heat the oil with the garlic,
breadcrumbs (and almonds, if using).
Fry for 5–10 minutes, stirring often until
golden. Stir through the lemon zest, if
using, and serve.

Tips:
To make 100g fresh breadcrumbs,
remove the crusts from about
2 thick slices of crusty bread
and rub into large crumbs.

Keep any leftovers in a sealed
container in the fridge for a few
days; they won't be quite as crisp
but will still be delicious.

SWEETCORN & CHEESE MUFFIN LOAF

I am a lifelong sweetcorn fan. I always have a tin in my rucksack for festivals or camping; it is best eaten straight out of the tin accompanied by a chunk of Cheddar cheese. Here these two meet in a loaf.

SERVES 8–10

175ml natural yogurt

2 eggs

90g unsalted butter, melted and cooled

198g tin sweetcorn, drained

bunch of spring onions, finely sliced

120g mature Cheddar cheese, grated

250g self-raising flour

2 teaspoons hot paprika

1 teaspoon baking powder

salt and freshly ground black pepper

Preheat the oven to 160°C/gas mark 4 and line a roughly 1kg loaf tin with greaseproof paper.

In a jug, whisk together the yogurt, eggs, butter, sweetcorn, spring onions and two-thirds of the cheese, then season. In a large bowl, mix together the flour, paprika and baking powder. Pour the jug contents into the bowl, stirring until combined.

Pour evenly into the prepared tin, sprinkle with the remaining cheese and bake for 45–55 minutes until golden, well risen and a skewer inserted into the centre comes out clean. Leave to cool in the tin for 10 minutes then pop on a wire rack to cool further. Best eaten the same day warm or cold, but will keep in an airtight container for about 4 days.

INDEX

THANK YOU.

Jamie, thank you for supporting and believing in me and for always listening while I wittered on about all things tinned for nearly a whole year! You're incredible and I feel very lucky to have you by my side.

Mum and dad, you've been there for everything. Thank you for your guidance, love and your endless recipe testing and tasting. Brodie, thank you for being full of encouraging words wherever you are and always being willing to be my guinea pig. Aunty Sarah, my creative council, I love bouncing ideas about with you over copious amounts of lentils and tea. Although you're not about to read this Granny Susan, thank you for planting the cooking seed, for always cooking around me, feeding and teaching me. You were such an amazing source of creativity and imagination. I'm sad I haven't been able to share this with you.

Thank you to Judith for giving me the opportunity to write this book – it was something I had always dreamt of, but never thought would happen to me. Isabel, thank you for being such a wonderful and patient editor. Lizzie, thank you so much for your gorgeous pictures and Louie for your beautiful props. Thank you Amélie for being a total gem. Steph, thank you, for all of your help. Louise, thank you for bringing it all together with your brilliant design. We Are Out of Office, thank you for your marvellous illustrations, I love them.

To all of my freelance work family, thank you so much for encouraging and believing in me and being totally fabulous.

Carolyn, thank you for being so understanding and patient while I totally took over the kitchen every day for months. To all the wondrous people who have tested recipes along the way, thank you – Jaz, Rio, Esther, John, Alice, Faye, Sophie, Starzy, Ags, Rachel (also thank you for your amaze proofing), Lindsay, Eleanor, Emily, Sera, Tazi and Rilwan. To all the tasters, thank you, too.

Lola's eyes were opened to the world of cookbooks, food photography and styling when she did work experience with Jamie Oliver and his food team. After school, she went to Glasgow School of Art and studied Fine Art Photography, though food continued to weave through her work there. After graduating she decided to return to the world of food styling and started working in the kitchens of cafes and bakeries while doing work experience with food stylists. She then progressed to assisting full time and then to being a stylist herself, expanding along the way into recipe testing and then writing.